# INSIGHTS INTO HR

Exploring the Human Aspect from Ground Zero

*The efficacy of any Human Resources Professional largely depends on effective contemplation and striking a finer balance between human resources and human relations at the workplace. One cannot sustain or flourish without the other.*

# INSIGHTS INTO HR

Exploring the Human Aspect from Ground Zero

Dhrubajyoti Majumdar

EXCELLER BOOKS™
A GLOBAL PRESS

Insights into HR
Exploring the Human Aspect from Ground Zero



Cover by Exceller Books using resources from Pixabay.com



ISBN: 978-81-19524-20-4

First published in India in 2024 by Exceller Books,
An imprint of GE Group
Address: G1, Dream Apartment, Degree College Road, Belgharia, Kolkata, 700056, India

EXCELLER BOOKS™
A GLOBAL PRESS

www.excellerbooks.com

# Dedication

*I humbly tribute the credit of this maiden work to my father Late Sri Aparesh Mozumdar, for his relentless guidance since childhood to date despite his absence in this physical world.*

*This book is a dream that I have committed to the little world for whom I live – an affectionate mother, a caring spouse and a loving daughter.*

# Acknowledgement

It is not very easy to recollect the names of those who inspired me knowingly or unknowingly and influenced me directly or discreetly. Too many names are on the list of inspirers and influencers.

Still, let me recall some of them who relatively and closely encouraged me to realise and unearth the potentiality, and I trust that my work will not dishearten them.

First and foremost, I would like to thank my father, who used to gift me a book as recognition for getting promoted to the next class, which I believe subconsciously conditioned my thought processes towards writing down this book.

I am thankful to my mother, spouse, and daughter, who helped me devote time to completing this noble work.

A few names must be mentioned, as without their encouragement, such a herculean task would have never been brought into the shape of a book. The names are as follows:

- Dr. (Professor) Shweta Jain – Dean & Program Head of ICFAI Business School (IBS), Jaipur and one of my closest friends who actively encouraged me to share experiences for the new talent pool of tomorrow.
- Late Meher H. Mehta – My first guide or 'first looking glass' into the corporate world, who nurtured me by putting his unparalleled faith in me. I can still recollect his one-word encouragement: 'Grow Up, Dhrubajyoti!' Sir, I have tried my best to be developed.

As I mentioned earlier, the list of influencers is quite long, and it is not easy to classify all their contributions into this book.

One of the finest mentors I was blessed with was Mr. N. Dharmarajan, ex-immediate supervisor in the present organisation. During the turbulent year of my life in 2018, when I first started jotting down thoughts, he used to encourage me, and still, I can recall his words: 'Your hidden potential found its way to the surface, so don't let it die.' Hopefully, I am justifying his statement.

There may be countless influencers directly and indirectly associated with me, and their process of thoughts inspired me to create something not only for the generation of today but also for the generation of tomorrow. A few names that keep on inspiring me are:

- Dr. Mrs. Tultul Aich Ghosh
- Dr. Debaprasad Chattopadhyay – Senior Professor & HOD – HR in the Globsyn Business School
- Priyanka Basu – Business Information Consultant Anthem Inc and my first summer intern.
- Swami Vedatitananda – Principal, Ramkrishna Mission Shilpamadira, Belur, Howrah
- All the admirers and colleagues

I sincerely apologise in advance if I miss any names, which is purely unintentional.

I always say that I am first an employee and then an HR professional. All my employees from all the organisations that I have ever worked for discreetly inspired me, and I strongly believe that this creation, to some extent, will reveal their day-to-day concerns, which I understood by being in their shoes and depicting them from the angle of an HR professional in my own language.

# Table of Contents

# Preface

It is a long thought-off aspiration and a dream that is triggered by two and a half decades of experience gathered across organisations engaged in diverse businesses. This book is the culmination of a series of thoughts, perspectives, and memories of the journey I have travelled so far, firstly as an employee and then as a human resource professional. The topics covered in the book, to an extent, may appear to be the antithesis of usual HR thoughts taught in colleges and widely propagated at the workplace because these are elucidations of various formal as well as informal discussions. Although I often incidentally entangled in a discussion, I sometimes viewed the situation either as a silent observer or observed from a bystander view[1]. Also, the depiction of various situations elaborated in the book may closely resemble the individual experiences of a few of the readers attached to human resources professions.

Ideally, this is not a book on Human Resources functions or strategies; rather, it is a perspective-oriented human resource handbook that dives deeper into the burning challenges that today's organisations and their human resource functions are facing. The book comprises several matrix diagrams to simplify the complexity of the challenges that I gathered during my career as an HR professional.

While reading the book, a few of the topics may seem elementary, but reading those topics can help any professional understand the basics and better internalise the rest of the subjects.

I suggest readers keep their patience until the end, glance through the chapters slowly, and try to reflect by comparing them with real-life scenarios. I am sanguine that after going through the book, the readers will surely locate some resemblances with their respective fields of work, and the objective of the book will be served.

It is quite tough to recollect all the interactions and conversations and writing them down as a book is quite challenging. Moreover, in human resources there is always a chance of a flip side which I have tried to highlight by acting as a devil's advocate[2]. Hence, readers in few occasions find certain situations which are actually depicted from the viewpoint of an employee. However, the author endeavours to help eminent readers understand, appreciate, and acknowledge the creation of human relations in every transaction between two or more individuals, irrespective of gender, caste, creed, seniority, or role.

I sincerely tried to make the management principles lucid to read and simple to understand for any individual, irrespective of their professional background. A few of the sacrosanct management philosophies have been discussed briefly; however, major emphasis has been put on their applications in actual workplaces.

The objective of the book is to understand the nitty-gritty of the relational aspects of human resources rather than focusing on the operational aspects of human resources, which can be taught at schools or learned from behavioural training or similar interventions based on the skill gap[3] of an individual.

Another objective is to share experiences with the future talent bank located at the campuses across demography by guiding them in understanding and accepting the differences of generation cohorts. It is high time for them to reflect upon the relational aspects of human resources that are flowing as an undercurrent within every profession, and a business cannot run in silos without creating value for the human capital[4], impacting both the top and bottom end of the business.

Lastly, the perspectives and experiences that have been discussed entirely evolved through individual viewpoints and any resemblances with any individuals are purely coincidental.

The objective of the book can only be met if you like to read it from the beginning and start practising a few of the tools and techniques in actual work scenarios which are tricky and have different emotions intertwined to make them more complex. I strongly urge every reader to go through the book with a mindset of accepting the truth, sometimes with a pinch of salt, and share their thoughts with me. It is the readers who can ultimately decide the success of a writer; hence, I keep my fingers crossed with the hope of success.

*Happy reading & let me take the privilege to nudge your inner human resource to rise and shine.*

# Chapter| 1

## Changing Focus to Change a Life

A few years ago, the punch line of a TV commercial caught my attention. The punch line of the commercial: 'It's your life, make it large.' Several of us saw that advertisement from a consumer's viewpoint. The eminent readers may be wondering how it is relevant to this chapter. Let me cast light on it.

While reflecting, it seemed to me that the meaning was quite significant without being judgmental of the product for which the advertisement was designed. In today's world, everyone is busy earning their livelihood; they are busy either with meetings, client calls, achieving targets, or balancing their personal life by following mundane routines as a spouse or a parent. Most of us might have experienced children growing up with the twinkling of an eye.

We are so engrossed in meeting or pursuing professional pursuits that the entity of 'I' is gradually extinct, and so is our purpose in life. Most of us might have forgotten to draw a sketch that we used to scribble through in our school days; perhaps we have not touched even our guitar, which we used to play during our college days, or we might have forgotten to walk around on a lush green field with our near ones because of occupational commitments or career rat-race. We are so influenced by the external world and are so busy responding to factors beyond our control that we do not know how to nourish our inner self on time, and it gradually dies. Let me take the opportunity to share a few thoughts, and I am sure that in the end, the readers will get a foundational understanding of how to live a purposeful life despite occupational pressure and personal commitments. Before diving deep, let me ask the readers a few simple questions about ourselves.

- *Have you ever felt the urge to figure out the purpose of your life apart from the creation of material affluence or position status?*
- *Have you ever developed any hobbies or interests apart from your technical subject?*
- *Have you ever felt the desire to invest in personal growth without considering any return from the organisation or society?*
- *If you perceive that you are stagnated within the organisation, have you ever felt the need to expand your horizon?*
- *How frequently do you appreciate others?*

If your answers are affirmative, i.e., yes to all the above questions, then you are all set to live a purposeful life, and there is little need to glance through this topic of discussion. However, those who feel otherwise must not leave this chapter in the middle of the road as it can help them better understand the purpose of life. Whenever someone is frustrated in life or is confused about finding out the reason to live, it is a common human tendency to blame the external environment. Instead of blaming external factors that are beyond our control, let us introspect inwardly to examine how we can create an environment for better and healthier living for ourselves.

❖ ***'Are we sincere enough to unlock our hidden potential or thrive to live with a purpose?'***

The perception of a purposeful life is usually camouflaged with either material possessions like a bigger condominium or luxury sedan, foreign travel, or extrinsic rewards like promotion, career growth, etc. However, the question is: Will these be sufficient to keep someone motivated forever, or is there something else that is still missing?

Ideally speaking, these are all desires rather than purposes, which, after gratification, are no longer relevant for leading a purposeful life. As soon as a new desire comes into our subconscious mind[5] and gradually imprints on our conscious mind, we get entangled and prefer to pursue it, and another cycle of desire starts shaping. In our country, there are only a few individuals who are more inclined towards philanthropic activities because the whole concept of reward is always attached to monetary terms.

Based on the set context, let us try to figure out and establish a link by answering the questions that were asked at the beginning of the discussion.

- *Have you ever felt the urge to figure out the purpose of your life apart from the creation of material affluence or position status?* – It is pitiful but blatantly true that very few people know why they live, and there is hardly anyone who can answer it. Every life has a greater purpose that we are never bothered to discover, and when it is discovered, it is too late. Therefore, friends, before it is too late, start searching for the purpose of developing new generations by sharing your experiences or attaching yourselves to social causes that can add value to society. Develop the mindset as a '***Giver***', and the environment will certainly change in your favour. A year ago, I got a chance to interact with an employee who used to offer lunch to the underprivileged during their marriage anniversary, which exemplifies a '*Giver*' attitude.
- *Have you ever developed any hobbies or interests apart from your technical subject?* – If you introspect, I am sure you will get the answer to this question. Like

your past hobbies that used to fascinate you, during official transactions of late, you can develop hobbies or any special interest; it may be story or poetry writing or any other hobby. It makes us feel proud that where each of us is running for outputs, there are at least some of us who are taking a keen interest in reading books on history or publishing books on poetry. Such hobbies will always keep you alive and can help you escape office gossip and mundane job or occupational stress.

- *Have you ever felt the desire to invest in personal development without considering any return from the organisation?* – It is a well-accepted fact that business and the social environment are changing rapidly. As a result, expectation levels are also changing on our professional and personal end. In HR, we have seen how dramatically the expectations of employees have changed over time. To equip with this radically changing internal and external environment, it is imperative for any individual to be abreast with respect to knowledge enhancement because ***'An investment in knowledge pays the best interest.'*** So, think beyond organisational training development opportunities, handpick pocket-friendly learning exposures, and start pursuing. Ask yourself, 'Have I added any new qualifications or new skills in the last year?' Do not always expect immediate benefits like sponsorship or promotion for a new qualification because most of the learning outcomes can eventually benefit by sharpening business acumen, equipping you to analyse in a better way.
- *If you perceive that you are stagnated within the organisation, have you ever felt the need to expand your horizon?* – An individual can be stuck with the

organisation without any growth due to various reasons. A few such reasons are within our control, but most of them are beyond our control. Individual perceptions of growth are also elusive, and the easiest practice is *object referral*[6], which is defining ourselves through external objects such as people, situations, possessions, etc. Such thinking can make any individual highly disengaged and demoralised as this sense of stagnation adversely affects our contribution toward achieving our own and organisational success. The only way to come out of this sense of stagnation can be to expand horizontally by nurturing new things or taking benefit of your learning, which you did earlier to expand your existing job, which we call 'Job Enlargement[7].' Zoom out of your existing job and then zoom in, and you will surely get the result - multi-tasking always pays.

- *How frequently do you appreciate others?* – Usually, people are hesitant to appreciate others but when it is a matter of criticism, they usually become overly critical. As a justification, it is commonly said that frequent appreciation will encourage individuals toward self-projection, and criticism will be a source of correction. But when you attend any training, how frequently are you appreciated by the training facilitator against each of your responses? Please remember that any act of appreciation for your child, colleague, subordinate, and even your superiors can create a positive vibe that can make the transaction mutually delightful. Even development feedback[8] can generate a positive result if it is shared in a manner of appreciation. You can easily try it in your home and test the efficacy of the feedback on your child. In an organisation, which is an extended family, leaders who are good at appreciation can easily gain acceptance, and their developmental feedback is positively taken by the subordinates.

In a nutshell, to understand the purpose of life, it is essential to be self-aware and very clear in differentiating the purpose from the desire of life and accordingly respond to internal and external factors. Individuals with higher levels of self-awareness are more likely to positively influence environmental factors, even if they are adverse. It is never too late to develop and unearth your limitless potential, utilise it to achieve the purpose of life, and, at the same time, share it with society to lead a life with purpose. After all, '*If the cranes can fly, why can't I?*'

# Chapter| 2

## Diving Deeper into the Ocean of Employee Attrition

The major and formidable challenge faced by any organisation today is managing employee turnover and retaining the right talent. Not only this, but manpower deployment, irrespective of performance category, can, sometimes, become a big challenge for the talent acquisition team to handle. Industries, irrespective of their size or nature of business, are tremendously suffering from a talent crunch due to the constant outflow of talented manpower, which hampers the organisation's operational efficiency and productivity.

Let us try to find answers to the following questions, which instantly crop up in the mind of any professional. Also, I shall try to find out the measurement yardstick and determinants of employee attrition[9], which will help the professionals effectively understand the subject matter they might come across in their organisations in one form or another.

- **What makes an employee leave an organisation?**
- **What measures can be initiated to control attrition and retain talent?**

Let us find out the answer to the first question, which will demystify the actual causes and effects of voluntary separation of the workforce prevalent in any industry.

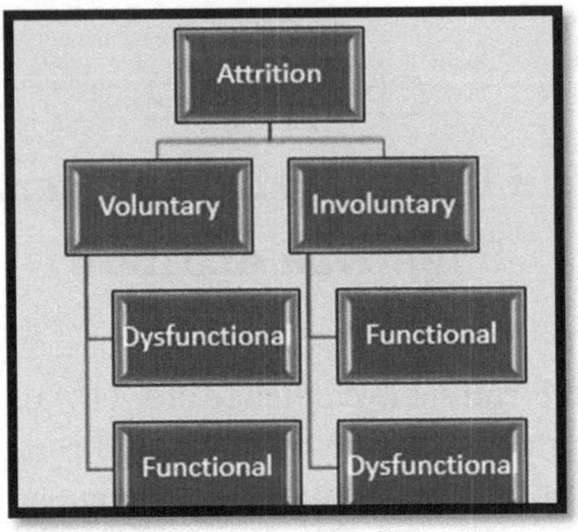


*Figure 2.1: Attrition Typologies*

*2.1. Involuntary Attrition*[10]

Let us reflect upon involuntary attrition. Usually, it is caused by retirement or superannuation[11], which is governed by the statutes of the nation. In the case of expatriate[12] employment, it can be caused by the termination of a contractual agreement. The same holds true for contractual employees and fixed-term advisors working after retirement with lump sum remuneration.

However, the most important and controversial aspect of involuntary attrition is planned interventions to reduce employee headcounts. Generally, the reduction of manpower manifests socio-economic and disruptive business scenarios that directly or indirectly influence business processes. Also, as part of the organisation's strategy for sustained operational excellence, downsizing or rightsizing can be an option to reduce hierarchical levels and/or abolish defunct positions, merge positions/departments, etc.

Involuntary attrition can also result from planned downsizing by pruning down non-performing human capital. This leads to better operational efficiency by cultivating a performance-driven culture across the organisation. During the pandemic, involuntary separation was observed in various forms across the globe to restrict or reduce headcounts and control the cost of overheads.

### *2.2. Circumstances of Dysfunctional Involuntary Attrition*

Usually, involuntary attrition is the last resort any organisation should initiate. However, there are certain contexts in which it does not satisfy the desired outcome for which it was initiated.

One of the key objectives of cutting down non-performing human assets is to promote meritocracy by elevating the performance benchmark of the organisation. However, when the demand for manpower is very high, or the industry is labour-intensive, an element of meritocracy is ideally to be instilled to keep the workflow moving.

Infusing fresh blood into the operation can also be an argument commonly propagated, but it is also subject to ***person-job (P-J fit)*** and ***person-organisation (P-O fit)*** fitment. Hence, without being ***P-O*** and ***P-J fit***, the performance of no new employee can be forecasted.

### *2.3. Remedial Measures*

To avoid human capital loss during the business downturn due to internal and external factors, one of the remedial measures practised widely by organisations since the COVID-19 pandemic is employment ***Furlough***[13]. The concept seems to be new, but it is widely practised in the information technology sector, which is called ***"Benching***[14]***"***.

As defined by Forbes, furlough is a mandatory leave of absence that employees are put on due to special circumstances faced by organisations. Such special circumstances include:

- Lack of budget or budget approval
- Insufficient work
- Slow economic condition
- Business reorganisation
- Unexpected disruptions, such as the COVID-19 lockdown

*Source: https://www.forbes.com/advisor/business/what-is-furlough/*

*2.4. Benefits of Furlough*

The best possible benefits of employment furlough from the viewpoint of an employer are:

- Access to the existing manpower accustomed to the organisation culture.
- Reducing the cost of overheads (both on account of salary and the cost of administration facilities) by partial payment of remunerations to furloughed employees.
- Less dependence on outside resources and additional recruitment costs coupled with the cost of settling down new employees within the new organisation, leading towards tougher performance predictability.
- Passing the message to the non-performers that without performance, employment is not fully guaranteed.
- Employment furlough can be beneficial from the perspective of an employee:
- It is not a loss of employment or layoff.
- Partial remuneration is guaranteed by the organisation.
- Once the business is back on track, regular employment can be restored.

- Hidden opportunities for moonlighting are there to bridge the income loss.

## *2.5. Voluntary Attrition*[15]

The causes and effects of voluntary attrition, on the contrary, are quite different and have far-reaching repercussions than involuntary attrition. To control voluntary attrition, one needs to be thorough enough to understand employee work psychology vis-à-vis prevailing market dynamics and what makes the employees satisfied in their work field and embedded with an organisation for a longer time.

Voluntary attrition can be categorised into two types:

- *Functional attrition*[16]
- *Dysfunctional attrition*[17]

### 2.5.1. Functional Attrition

It is said that 3-5% attrition is good for an organisation, but beyond that, it is a matter of concern depending on the industry. Usually, it is always better for actively disengaged employees to leave the organisation since they are not contributing but spreading the message of negativity for others to follow.

There are various reasons contributing to functional attrition. A few of the reasons, though not exhaustive, are as follows:

- Non-compatibility with Person-Job and Person-Organisation,
- Poor inclination towards upskilling[18] or reskilling[19],
- Disciplinary issues and lack of commitment,
- Sticking to the obsolete role,
- Repeated poor performance despite feedback,
- Sustained health and psychological issues.

Despite the reasons mentioned above, due diligence should be adopted in formulating the retention strategy[20] based on the role and skill set requirement. The skillset can easily be replenished by way of recruitment, and healthy employee turnover is welcome.

### 2.5.2. Dysfunctional Attrition

On the other side, employee turnover, which is dysfunctional for the organisation, affects the organisation on several fronts. It has a huge cost impact as the skill set is not easily available in the market. However, one relevant question may arise in the mind of a reader: Can all the attritions be controlled? Unfortunately, the answer is NO. Some of the employee turnovers are unavoidable in nature and beyond the control of any organisation, despite its all-good intention to keep such employees on board. A few of the issues for which employees are opting for resignation are mentioned below:

- Compensation and benefits
- Management of philosophy
- Locational constraints
- Lack of work-life balance
- Pursuing higher studies
- Initiation of own business
- Overseas assignment
- Lack of career advancement
- Lack of performance feedback
- Post-marriage relocation with spouse

Avoidable turnover can be controlled through a well-designed employee retention strategy and engagement plan. However, before proceeding further, let us measure employee turnover and factors that affect voluntary attrition. Employee attrition can be ascertained using the formula of:

$$\text{Attrition rate} = \frac{\text{Number of employees left the organisation}}{\text{Average headcounts of employees of the year}}$$

Capturing employee attrition is not an easy task, and neither is it simple to arrest as traditionally propagated by industry experts. The relationship between the employer and the employee is partially governed and regulated through the appointment letter or employment policies and procedures. However, a substantial part of employment is mutual understanding and implicitly tied through what is called a psychological contract. Any minor lapse or modification into it may disturb this contract and foment anti-establishment feelings among the employees, which can either be expressed or remain silent but ramified into silent quit.

Therefore, it is pertinent to understand the various element of retention and their greater implications in successfully managing the employee life cycle.

### *2.6. Understanding Employee Retention Strategy*

It is important for the HR department to minimise the loss of human capital as a part of its yearly goals. It is equally important for the operations to understand the need for the retention of human resources for operational efficiency and to ensure business success.

The relative importance of formulating a retention strategy can be viewed through the 2 x 2 matrix, in which the independent variable is considered the number *of Attritions* and plotted against the horizontal axis, and the dependent variable is treated as *the Importance of Retention* plotted against the vertical axis. Let us now reflect upon four unique situations and the desired strategy for retention.

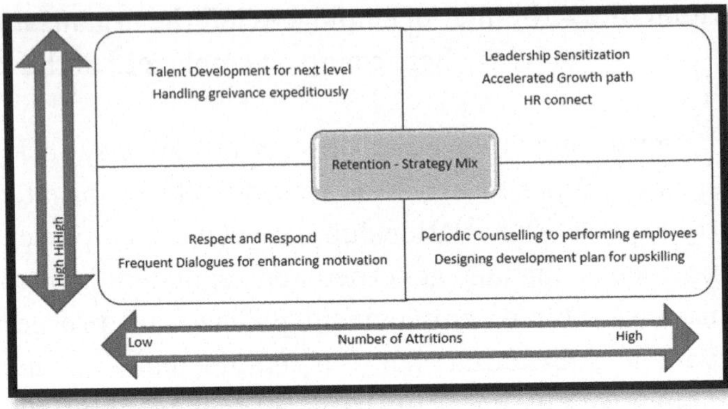


*Figure 2.2: Retention Strategy Mix*

### 2.6.1. High Retention Requirement and High Attrition Numbers

In today's world of opportunities, retaining the right talent is indeed a big challenge for industrial organisations. It can further be aggravated when the employee expectations are not seemingly clear or idiosyncratic. Critical talents are generally classified into this category, and the requirement for a robust retention strategy is a must. Erosion in the pool of critical talents actively dampens organisational performance. Such attrition can act as a two-way sword. It will drain out well-developed and time-tasted talent from the organisational talent pool, and recruiting the critical talent with desired skill sets is time-consuming and requires a higher *Turnaround Time (TAT)*[21]. Therefore, the retention of talent is not the only headache for the HR team to act upon. However, prior sensitisation should be given to business and operation teams so they can take the utmost precautions well before the actual occurrence of attrition.

Employees equipped with key skills and superior performance standards develop high career aspirations from the organisation over time. Sometimes, they may find a gap between their aspirations and the actual position, which ultimately drives them to quit the organisation. Therefore, for accelerated career growth, a necessary policy must be in place to prevent these talents from leaving the organisation. The three key strategies can play a pivotal role in retaining critical talents. They are as follows:

- Leadership sensitisation
- Frequent connections by HR are needed to understand the aspirations and shattering dreams, if any.
- Designing accelerated career growth for the right talents based on sustained performance.

2.6.2. Low Requirement of Retention and High Attrition Numbers

In general, organisations are falling in love with talented employees with lesser tenure of employment and keep on running till they move out of hand. It is a usual tendency for any organisation to focus all the developmental efforts on the talents and undermine silent performers. ***Quiet quitting***[22] is commonly evidenced in this phase and can be a potential threat for any organisation engaged in the process, assembly line or construction engineering operations wherein the scope and involvement of human resources are potentially higher.

*2.7. Decoding the Money as a Factor of Attrition*

Financial consideration is the most common factor affecting employee psychology regarding whether to stay in or leave an organisation. Managers at senior or middle management levels are more attracted to fringe benefits[23] or perks like performance incentives[24]/retention bonuses[25], stock option schemes[26], and medical facilities. However, for entry-level executives, as of now, net take-home salary, cash components, or telephone reimbursement plays a pivotal role in employee retention.

The compensation policy across industries is officially implemented to keep salary and benefits confidential. However, it is the most discussed subject-matter among employees. The peer groups comprising of members with similar ages and experience usually compare themselves against financial parameters like salary hikes, performance ranking (sometimes based on mere perception), faster promotions, etc. It has been observed in several cases that such type of peer group comparison leads to frustration, burnout, consequent disengagement and attrition.

### 2.7.1. Low Requirement of Retention and Low Numbers of Attrition

I would like to ask a simple question: How many people are there who are leaving the organization and their requirement is also low? It will not be an easy question to answer because these populations can include employees who downgraded thanks to forced distribution[27] or the bell curve fitment process of evaluation. Despite the downgrading, these populations are finding it difficult to exit the organisation due to a zone of comfort in a familiar work atmosphere.

Another constituent of this category of employees is the bulk hires from campuses who usually find it tough to acclimate to the non-familiar atmosphere and work pressure to manage the work and life as per their expectations. However, the consistent exodus of campus hires often marks a question against employer branding, and therefore, it requires special attention. In the majority of industries, there is a huge influx of the Gen Z[28] workforce in the form of trainees (management/ engineering/ apprentice), and a few of the reasons for leaving the employment are:

- Work-life balance.
- Higher studies
- New businesses or start-ups[29]
- Lack of purposeful job assignment
- Dampening learning opportunities
- Fun at the workplace
- Working closer to the family
- Flexible working hours
- Opportunities for ideation
- Faster query resolution

It is pertinent to mention here that the HR team should dive deeper to ascertain the triggering factors leading towards voluntary employment termination. An organisation must take care of all the above factors (not an exhaustive one) to ensure job satisfaction[30] for a moderate period.

### 2.7.2. Higher Requirement of Retention and Low Numbers of Attrition

From the point of view of an organisation, perhaps the employees plotted against this quadrant can be termed ***solid citizens***[31]. These employees are fully indoctrinated with the organisation's culture and contribute without high aspirations. Employees who have spent the majority of their career within one organisation and have grown through thick and thin can demonstrate the ***organisation's citizenship behaviour*** (OCB)[32]. Since the potential risk of loss in this category of employees is reasonably high and the cost of replacement is still higher, it is always suggested that they should be ring-fenced by laying down a detailed development plan for career growth.

Like the quiet quitters, this category of employees can leave the organisation once they feel like taking it for granted by the employer. It is always better for the HR team to handle their concern or grievances expeditiously to make them feel psychologically safe. Though the attrition rate at this level is reasonably low and employees are comparatively senior in age as well as in position, the reasons behind exit are also different as below:

- Company policies
- Feeling stagnated and obsolete
- Lack of psychological safety at the workplace
- Changing work climate and culture
- Compromised work ethics.
- Undue stress at work and harassment

Solid citizens are employees who continuously support their leaders in achieving their goals; therefore, it is the principal obligation of any organisation to take care of the well-being of the employees by addressing their concerns that can emanate from the above-mentioned triggering factors of dissatisfaction.

### *2.8. Why Is Attrition So Costly for Any Organisation?*

In the previous sections, the context has already been set, and by now, it is easier to understand the cost implications of any unhealthy attrition. The cost of attrition can be both intrinsic and extrinsic for the organisation.

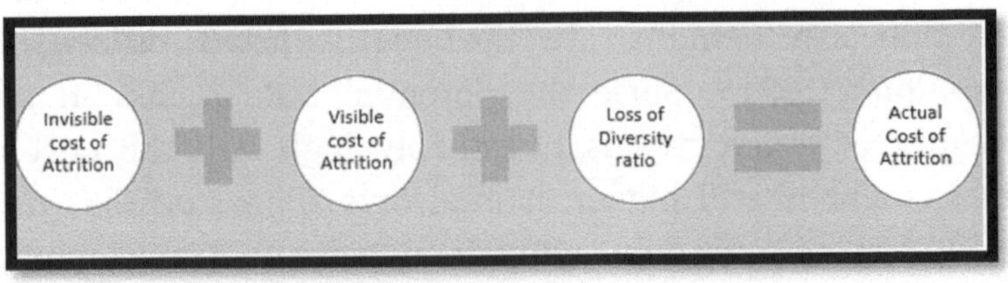


*Figure 2.3: Equation of Attrition*

Every voluntary attrition is painful for an organisation and for the HR teams. However, the invisible loss is often underestimated due to the non-availability of objective evidence. Since the organisation is a conglomeration of people with diverse interests, the background and belief system is organic in nature. Hence, any dysfunctional loss of human capital by way of attrition can add to the intrinsic loss for an organisation in the form of:

- Erosion in employee loyalty[33] as an employer of choice
- Erosion in market share by draining out information.
- Market rumours about culture
- Rehiring of boomerang employees[34]

The above list depends more on the industry and the role of employees leaving the organisation. Nevertheless, such cost is intrinsic and capturing it in monetary terms has never been widely practised by any organisation.

Secondly, the visible cost of attrition is manifold, and since the data is available, it draws more attention for HR analytics professionals to dig down more into the factors responsible for the attrition to predict beforehand and prescribe the way out.

Finally, diversity, equity, and inclusion are three closely linked values held by many organisations that work to support different groups of individuals, including people of different races, ethnicities, religions, abilities, genders, and sexual orientations.
https://www.mckinsey.com/featured-insights/mckinsey-explainers/what-is-diversity-equity-and-inclusion#/

To sustain in the competition as an employer of choice, the majority of the organisations are promoting DEI[35] by embedding diversity, equity and inclusion in hiring activities and HR policies. A few of the best practices followed by the reputed organisations are:

- Promoting women into leadership roles

- The inclusion of female employees in operational and front-line roles by increasing campus hiring
- Enhancing the gender diversity ratio[36]
- Policy and procedural support for greater gender inclusivity
- Exploring growth avenues for female employees
- Gender-specific roles
- Ongoing commitment of the organisation to any violation under the POSH[37] act

Therefore, it is crystal clear that maintaining and nurturing a culture suitable for DEI attracts costs to the organisation in the form of recruitment, training, and maintaining a proper gender diversity ratio.

Therefore, the exit of a female employee can adversely affect the diversity ratio, and replacement costs with suitable skill sets are reasonably higher than those of their male counterparts.

In today's scenario, manpower is treated as an asset; therefore, attrition of any kind has a huge cost impact on an organisation, and it affects the overall image of the employer. The cost of attrition can be trifurcated into three heads:

- Replacement Cost[38]
- Exit Cost[39]
- Operational Cost[40]

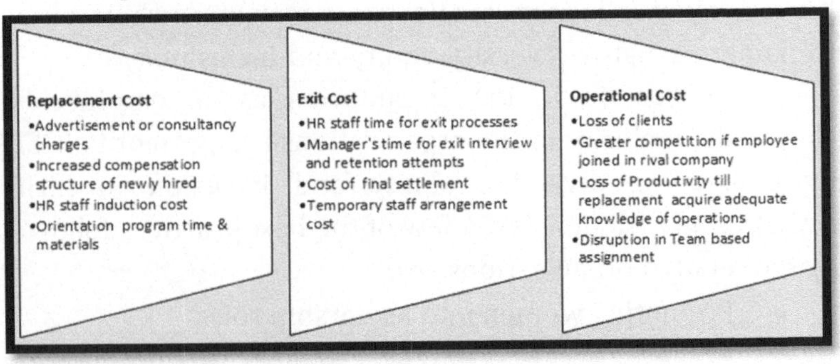


*Figure 2.4: Attrition Cost*

By now, the readers of this chapter have already got a fair idea about employee attrition – its type, causes and impacts on an organisation either directly or indirectly.

Can employee attrition be controlled? And if yes, then how? Attrition can be largely controlled through a robust retention strategy with an emphasis on employee development, reward and employee engagement. A well-developed and executed retention strategy should focus on employee retention not only when the job market is good but also when the job market is in bad shape, as there is no dearth of job opportunities for top-performing staff equipped with critical skill sets. Let us now examine the various measures that a company can initiate to mitigate employee attrition.

- **Recruitment Policy**: A well-designed recruitment plan that focuses on putting the right person in the right position can mitigate the chances of post-recruitment grievances of an employee regarding job content and salary structure.
- **Induction Plan**: Each employee, irrespective of position and grade, requires some time to get accustomed to the company norms, policies, and practices. This requirement of an employee can be addressed through an induction plan. Also, initial orientation has an effect on the improvement of Employee Value Proposition[41]. It has been observed that a good number of employees prefer to leave a company due to initial disruption in their socialisation process. It is quite pertinent that all employees mandatorily go through a series of induction processes to get themselves accustomed to the system.
- **Well Chalked out Reward Policy**: One of the critical factors that constitute employee attrition is lack of

career growth and dissatisfaction related to the reward mechanism of the organisation. Though it is not fully possible to satisfy the employees, particularly in this aspect, such dissatisfaction can be mostly addressed through a reward policy that has clarity on performance measurement and a clear linkage between performance and career growth. It is essential to have a performance-driven culture in an organisation, which should always encourage good performance and, at the same time, segregate poor performers for necessary counselling and feedback. Reward policy should always focus on churning talents and can obviously be used as a retention technique.

- **Opportunities for Training & Development**: Any employee, irrespective of their expertise or grade or gender, joins an organisation with a specific set of skills. However, over a period of time, some of the skills need continuous upgradation (e.g. information technology) to cater to the growing demand for the job content and help an employee to be well positioned for further growth and employability. Hence, opportunities for skill enhancement certainly act as a tool for employee retention. In some of the organisations, there is a provision of partial reimbursement of tuition fees to employees who complete programs like BE/MBA from reputed colleges and B-Schools. Linking employee development with retention strategies has a positive impact on overall workforce retention. Employees with desired talents need to be fostered to create a next-level leadership pool. The design and implementation of various leadership programs help employees prepare themselves to undertake the next higher position with greater responsibilities and a wider span of control.

- **Employee Communication**: An open-door communication policy paves the way towards employee satisfaction by making them feel worthwhile. As a retention tool, the employee-connect program can help immensely by encouraging employees to share their feelings and concerns related to their job content, career growth, and even any personal issues that may have an impact on their work performance or relationships. Such types of open communication can unearth facts on employee attrition and help management develop policies on employee retention. Such interaction helps an employee understand their company, and several misconceptions may be abolished.
- **Caring Work Environment**: Gone are the days when employees only worked to earn their minimum livelihood. In the post-globalisation era, we have found that employees' aspirations are increasing. Work is no longer a profession, but it is something more. The working environment has a direct impact on the work behaviour of an employee. So, to retain the employees, the work content should not only be interesting but also have some fun value. An employee-friendly work atmosphere is also becoming a major tool for attracting and retaining employees with sustained performance.
- **Effective Employee Engagement**: Employee engagement can be defined as a degree to which an employee is emotionally bonded to their organisation and passionate about their own work. Effective employee engagement programs can help an

organisation largely ensure employee retention. In recent times, most professional organisations have undertaken some sort of employee engagement program. Some of the engagement drives, though not an exhaustive one, are as follows:

- **Employee Referral Program**: Employees can be treated as the chief advocate of the company. Hence, instead of hiring from an external source, employees can source a candidate using their own network. If the candidate is selected and works for the company for at least 6 months, the employee who referred the candidate can be awarded a referral bonus.
- **Buddy Fixation:** In the initial days of joining, to hold the hand of a new entrant, a buddy or mentor can be chosen for an employee or a group of such new employees. Generally, a buddy or mentor can be from the same department and should have fairly good knowledge about the company and its operations.
- **Reward & Recognition Program:** Recognition programs like "Employee of the Year," "Best Performer Award" or "Award for Long Service" can have a positive impact on the sustained performance of an employee.
- **Meeting with Senior Management Team**: In some organisations, newly inducted staff are required to undergo a series of processes, and meeting with the senior management team is one of them. It actively boosts their morale during their initial journey in the organisation.
- **Work-Life Balance**: Most of the IT/ITES companies have flexible working hours and "work from home[42]" systems. This encourages employees

to work effectively and helps them maintain the work-life balance. Reputed IT companies like Google offer separate crèche facilities for female employees having kids. This also ensures emotional attachment towards an organisation. In some companies, anniversary breaks are offered to help employees spend a day with their dear ones.

However, engagement tools that can be used as retention techniques may differ from organisation to organisation based on various aspects, such as the culture or core values of the organisation, the nature of the business, workforce diversity, gender ratio, etc. Before implementing such tools, a proper survey needs to be done.

In 21st-century globalised India, employee retention has become a major challenge, and the time has come to respond effectively to this challenge by identifying and analysing the root cause of attrition and developing a suitable strategy focusing on effective implementation and subsequent monitoring.

Last but not the least, not only HR managers, but also all line managers should play a crucial part in identifying the talent and its retention for a greater organisational interest. In a nutshell, without a well-designed retention plan, it is not possible for any organisation to enjoy sustained growth in the business over a longer period.

# Chapter| 3

## Balancing Business and People – A Unique Ballgame for HR

During their career journey as human resource professionals, HR practitioners quite often come across qualitative statements that can either be 'HR is ok' or 'HR is bad' or maybe in absolute or relative terms. Even though the statement is highly subjective, it needs serious contemplation. Usually, such remarks are passed by business leaders, sometimes line staff, and workers. Most of the time, qualitative comments catch little attention since it is a phenomenon of any human being to play safe by passing the buck to a relatively vulnerable group. Any employee or stakeholder can appreciate HR upfront, but the question is: What are those deep-rooted factors that are posing a hindrance to people recognizing the people of HR?

This topic of discussion is based on a specific observation shared by one of the business leaders about a senior HR professional, which has compelled me to go for a deep dive from the perspective of a general employee.

Despite the assumption that the ***'HR job is thankless by its very nature,'*** let us highlight some of the comments that both internal and external stakeholders[43] are focusing upon. These observations are mostly held across industries and levels of hierarchy.

- ***Responsiveness*** – It has been observed that several times, people find it useless to approach the HR department with a preconceived notion of not getting a straightforward answer. Vague replies like 'Let you know' or 'will check and revert' made employees more frustrated and agonized. This is probably why employees feel much more comfortable discussing issues and concerns within themselves. It is quite true that line staff are well aware of policies and loopholes and whether there is any change in employment/benefits policy. However, discussing policies through the grapevine[44] often leads to misconception and confusion; nevertheless, the grapevine is a rich source of discussion on issues impacting the terms of employment contracts.

- ***Patient Listening*** – How many times does an HR pick up the calls of a common employee with a smile on their face and listen carefully to the concerns and issues of an employee? The answer is probably 'no.' Therefore, slowly but steadily, contact and bonding are loosened up, and to protect the position, the inclination is to lean toward the management. *In my own words, sales professionals are paid for pushing the client to purchase the product, while human resources professionals are paid for carefully listening to the people, understanding their problems and extending support to them.* The product here is a service that is difficult to measure from the perspective of a shop floor employee. Therefore, utmost importance is required to deal with the issues and concerns. An important measurement criterion is how the solution provider deals with the employee and the quality and timeliness of solutions.
- ***Misconception of a Solution Provider*** – Most HR people are suffering from a preconceived notion that people are approaching them to solve their issues and problems. However, this is not always true at all. Employees may often approach HR just to vent out

their steams of agony or seek suggestions or clear confusion on various policies and regulations governing employment contracts, despite being fully aware of the fact that HR cannot solve all the problems and issues. Hence, a scenario appears in which before the employee speaks out, the HR personnel starts a conversation with preconceived notions about the problems for which he/she is approached. This gives the employee the feeling: 'I have not been heard by HR.' As an HR professional, it is not always mandatory to offer a solution, but listening to the issue with due empathy is the most important part.

- ***Position Consciousness*** – Let me take this opportunity to ask how many of you are feeling uncomfortable while interacting with the HR manager, and most of you will answer that you feel uncomfortable. The principal cause of such discomfort is that most of you have the preconceived idea that when someone is holding the chair in the HR department, he or she must be position-conscious and easily become judgemental towards employee issues and concerns. In many organizations, employees working in the human resources department work separately to protect confidentiality protocols, which, in turn, develops in them a high-handed behavioral pattern dealing with employee matters.
- ***Identity Crisis*** – Particularly in traditional owner-driven organizations, the HR managers are not treated equally with other line managers by business leaders, and usually, leaders perceive the HR function as a cost function that erodes profitability. In some organizations, HR means a department that satisfies the whims and fancies of business and handles industrial relations or employee grievances beyond

the control of line managers. The HR team often does not have any other options but to nod their head and obey the directives. So, in such cases, it is tough for HR professionals to walk the extra mile for their staff as they themselves are in an identity crisis, even when it comes to conveying the message to staff. The possible reason for the dilemma in making decisions lies in the crisis of identity and/or maintaining equal distance between employer and employees.

To examine the matter deeply, the undersigned is introducing a 2 X 2 Matrix model wherein the likelihood of specific behavior can be understood or be interpreted by considering the two factors:

- *Concern for the Business (CfB)*
- *Concern for the Employees (CfE)*

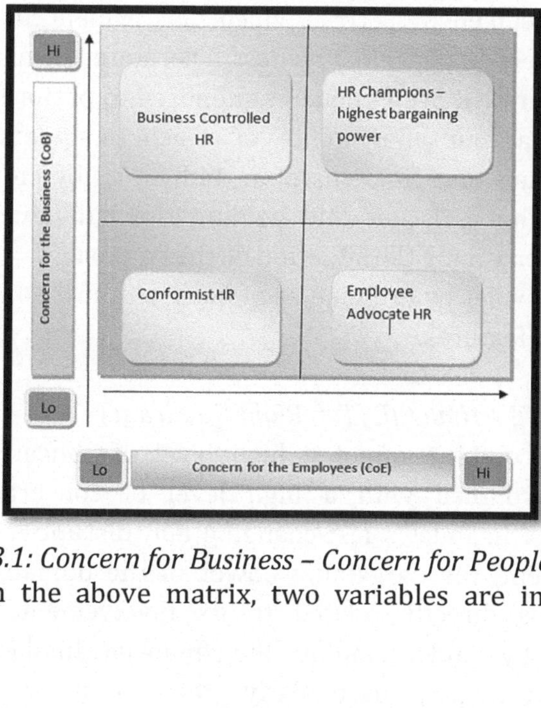


*Figure 3.1: Concern for Business – Concern for People: Matrix*

In the above matrix, two variables are introduced, namely:

- Concern for the Business (CfB): In today's scenario, every HR is supposed to be a torch bearer of the business, and therefore, their involvement is more in the business areas like profitability, return on investment (ROI)[45], and Return on Talent Employed (ROTE)[46]. As a business partner, the role of HR has significantly changed and KRA/ KPIs[47] have also undergone major changes due to the inclusion of financial metrics in place of qualitative statements of measurement. In a nutshell, the human resource function breaks down the silo and is inclined towards ensuring the business interest.
- Concern for the Employees (CfE): One of the basic competencies required for a human resource professional to work effectively is strong people orientation coupled with a high level of Emotional Intelligence (EI)[48], which is evidenced through interpersonal effectiveness. Therefore, to some extent, every HR professional is supposed to perform the role of a counsellor, guide, or coach to understand the issues and concerns of an individual by empathizing with the issues and guiding the individual toward overcoming the situation or the context.

Now, let us examine each quadrant of the matrix and its specific features.

### *3.1. High CfB + High CfE (Top Right Quadrant)*

It is the combination of a high level of concern for the business coupled with a high level of concern for the employees. In today's fast-changing and disruptive business environment, the bargaining power of the human resource function is directly related to its involvement with the business by understanding the financial implications of people strategies, particularly their cost implications.

Therefore, the bargaining power of HR will be more as they are aware of the businesses. The HR business partners are favorably placed to influence the business by making changes to people-related policies and acting as *HR champions*.

*3.2. Low CfB + High CfE (Lower Right Quadrant)*

This combination is characterized by a higher concern for people and a lower concern for the business process. Usually, at the transactional level of handling, people are often inclined toward human resources professionals focusing on individual or group requirements to ensure higher job satisfaction or mitigate employee grievances. Particularly at the regional or shop floor level, the HR teams mainly focus on maintaining the occupational health and hygiene of employees and workers. Therefore, the focus of HR on people engagement by improving job satisfaction is much higher than their focus on business. Far from the business, local HR managers are playing the crucial role of *Employee Advocates*[49].

*3.3. Low CfB + Low CfE (Lower Left Quadrant)*

To reflect properly, let me ask the readers whether they are working in human resources function or attached to any other profession. The question is: At the beginning of your career, what types of assignments were you associated with? The answer will be making cold calls, preparing Excel sheets with scores of data, or, at best, designing a last-minute presentation for the boss with a lot of data and clipart. As an entry-level human resource officer, someone needs to do all routine jobs like entry into the employee database and personal file updating.

Usually, little scope is provided to an entry-level employee to understand business and an employee. The sole competency for success in the entry-level position is smart work to take care of the mundane job as a '*Conformist*[50] *HR.*'

*3.4. High CfB + Low CfE (Top Left Quadrant)*

As we discussed earlier, the question raised on the responsiveness of the human resource department often adversely affects the image of the department and leads to unwarranted escalation of employee issues. This is evidenced when the concern for the business is deeper than the concern for the people, and the HR organization is vulnerable to business pressures or unable to handle them with due effectiveness. There is a high chance that HR personnel will gradually become unresponsive toward the people cause, particularly when such causes collide with business interests. In this scenario, the business usually controls the HR functions, and the people's orientation of the organization also depends on the people's vision of the business leaders.

Human beings are one of a unique kind, comprised of the heart and mind, which can feel emotions and translate them through the brain. They can also segregate good emotions from bad ones, cherish the good ones and forget the bad ones. The good emotions generated through a positive interaction carry a positive image of the people. In human resources function, we are always an HR round the clock, and every action is watched through the lens of subjectivity. Hence, it is always advisable to exercise humility coupled with empathy and emotional intelligence to walk the extra mile for the cause of the employees toward higher customer delight to discover a true leader within you.

# Chapter| 4

## Decision Makers & Decision Takers – The Paradoxical Interface

Organizational decisions usually impact either the top end of business or the bottom end or both. Hence, the decisions that impact the top end of the business are termed strategic decisions, and the decisions that impact the bottom end are termed operational-level decisions.

Any decision that affects the input, process and output of any organization is led by the top leadership and percolates below. Therefore, there is a possibility that the looking glass used by the stakeholders at both ends of business differs considerably in view or approaching the context under which a decision is required to be made or taken. On several occasions, line managers implement or take the decisions mandated from the above without owning the decisions; hence, implementation can be half-hearted, and its efficacy remains questionable. Paradoxically, local decisions taken by line functions several times are not backed well by the decision makers, which can ultimately squeeze away the zeal of initiating the decisions of the line functions and even if the outcome is reasonably good, it is never brought to the limelight to senior management level.

***Decision-makers*** are the people or a group of people responsible for all the business decisions and accountable to the shareholders, internal and external customers, and other businesses. Decision-makers are empowered to design and formulate as well as implement the decisions across the organization for the achievement of both short- and long-term goals of the organization and stakeholders associated with it. On the other hand, ***decision-takers*** are the people or a group of people responsible for understanding, disseminating and implementing the decisions at the operational end and ensuring the efficacy of decisions locally by owning them. Therefore, henceforth, ***stakeholders of decisions*** will be used to denote both the stakeholders of decision-making and decision-taking.

Decision-making and decision-taking appear to be almost synonymous, and there are strong possibilities of misinterpretation. However, there are a few thick lines of differences. Predominantly, unlike the smaller organizations, usually, in large organizations, stakeholders responsible for decision-making and decision-taking are different sets of people. Another difference is that the decisions formulated by decision-makers are based on holistic macro assumptions pertaining to the organization and the business environment without much consideration of the local business dynamics. As a result, on several occasions, decisions that are percolated towards the operational level are unable to secure proper acceptance and ownership, and it becomes quite tough to implement them.

The reason for the decision debacle can be manifold; however, a two-way communication to understand and appreciate both micro and macro factors is imperative for all stakeholders. Otherwise, there can be a lack of clarity provided to the line management responsible for implementing the decisions. An ideal example can be evidenced at regional level hiring in the senior profile, in which the entire hiring process is completed without any prior communication to the local human resource team and local business leaders, which may lead to an unwelcoming experience of on boarding. Though the example is a generalized anecdote, there may be several cogent reasons

behind the non-disclosure of leadership hiring to the local management. However, it is always better to communicate the decisions well beforehand to avoid unpleasant situations.
Also, it is worth mentioning that the involvement of stakeholders in any decision-making process can differ significantly, and it is reflected by the quality of decisions and subsequent outcomes. The level of competence at both ends of the business leaders can play a crucial role by showcasing integrity to own the decision and extending support to the decision-takers to customize decisions based on local business dynamics.

Finally, the credibility of decision-making stakeholders is the key to the success of any strategic decision. Credibility is the major binding force of communication and competence, though according to the **Great Place to Work**[51] **R** institute, the latter two elements are the components of credibility. The degree to which decisions are in sync with the value and the belief of the stakeholders can be denoted as credibility of action, which means a lot for the follower to own the decision in letter and spirit.

### *4.1. 3C Disconnect – Example from World War II*

A classic case of disconnect between decision-maker and decision-taker can be figured out in the history of World War II. It was the clash between two legendary personalities: the great dictator of all time, ***Adolf Hitler***, and the decorated war hero of the German 7th Infantry Division, Field Marshall ***Erwin Rommel*** (*nicknamed Desert Fox*). The conflict of both had ultimately forced the German military might to quit the North Africa mission after a defeat in the war at ***El-Alamein*** in Libya in 1942 led by the Allied troops. Both were engaged in a bitter conflict, which resulted in the defeat of the German military might.

> ***A classic case of this disconnection between decision maker and decision taker can be figured out in the history of the World War II. The clash between legendary dictator Adolf Hitler and decorated war hero of the 7th German Infantry division Field Marshall Erwin Rommel which had eventually forced the German military might to quit the North Africa mission after the defeat in the war of the El-Alamein in Libya 1942 lead by the allied troop.***

It was no less than a story with full of pathos associated with it. It was a tale of a capable decision-taker who repeatedly denied taking independent decisions by the decision-maker (*Hitler*). Diverting the valuable resources elsewhere on the European war front caused a shortage in supply lines during the war of El-Alamein, which compelled Rommel to lose the battle. The tragic part of the story was that Rommel was nurtured and elevated to the senior rank by Hitler, and once Rommel commented, **"[Hitler] is extraordinarily friendly to me."** Despite the tussle between the two legendary figures, surprisingly, goals of Nazi supremacy were found to be common, but the means of achieving them were considerably different. The tragic episode continued since Rommel was falsely accused and faced trial for perpetrating the conspiracy for the assassination of Hitler on 8th September 1944, which forced Rommel to commit suicide, bringing an infamous end to the life of a decorated war hero!

It was an instance of blockage in communication between two leaders side by side, a gap in competence and a poor show of credibility as a leader to stand beside in a time of need. Hence, instead of harnessing the common goal of the nation, both were involved in the dysfunctional conflict[52].

The anecdote may have generated a few questions in the mind of the eminent readers, and greater will be a chance that the questions are in and around the below factors:

- ***Level of communication among the Decision Stakeholders***
- ***Level of the perception of competence among the Decision Stakeholders***
- ***Level of credibility of the Decision Stakeholders***

In the next sections, an effort will be made to unravel the interconnectivity of ***Communication - Competence - Credibility*** factors that directly contribute to the successful decision-making or decision-taking process.

Since the anecdote is interconnected with the topic of discussion, reference to the same will be taken intermittently.

### *4.2. Framework of 3C - Communication - Competence - Credibility*

It will be rather a utopian reflection that all the decisions permeated from the top will never face any challenge and will be well-accepted and implemented at the operational level with greater efficacy. Though there are numerous factors and facets associated with the disconnection among the decision stakeholders (both those who are making the decisions and those who are taking the decisions), there are three principal factors that mostly contribute towards the success or debacle of any decisions designed from the top and implemented at operative level. These are known as 3Cs, namely:

- *Communication*
- *Competence*
- *Credibility*

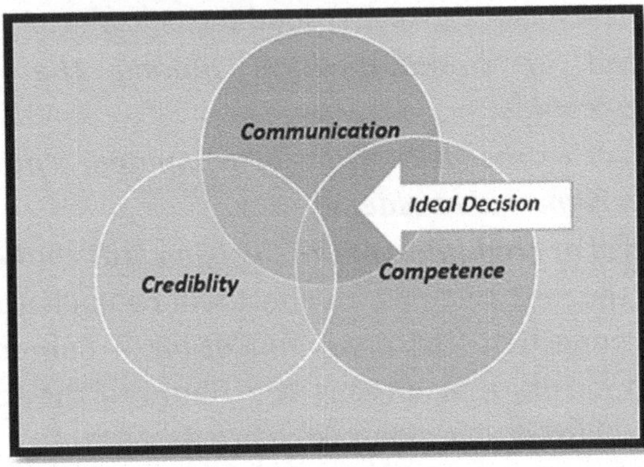


*Figure 4.1*

According to figure I, 3Cs are intertwined with one another and synergistic in nature. Any decision successfully rolled out from the top and implemented with greater acceptance at the bottom end of the business must have followed ***3Cs, i.e. Communication, Competence and Credibility.***

*4.3. Figure I – 3 Cs of Decision-Making and Decision-Taking*

Each of these factors is to be critically examined, and how each factor affects or distorts the decisions needs to be understood from the viewpoint of both stakeholders associated with it.

4.3.1. First C – Communication

Though two-way communication is one of the elements of credibility *(by Michael Burchell et al.),* it is the single most important block that can make or break the decision-making process. Therefore, it is imperative to ponder a few sections on communication.

If the earlier anecdote can be referred to, the leader's unparalleled supremacy led to a situation where decisions were never discussed or reflected upon rather than implemented. One-way communication from decision-maker to decision-taker made it increasingly difficult to understand the reason or strategy behind the decision and then disseminate it down the line for effective implementation.

Ideally, any strategic decisions must be preceded by the creation of familiarity in both the top and the bottom end of the organization coupled with a fair understanding of their causation. To create such a transparent climate, the decision-making authorities should be the forerunners and play a crucial role by providing informative and accessible communication without judgment.

It is also equally important to know how communication flows across hierarchies. Two-way communication is suggested to be maintained, especially before the formulation of any strategy or decision. Understanding the ground reality by the decision-makers is a pivotal ingredient for the formulation of any decision, as the whole process can be neither created nor implemented in silos.

Therefore, accessible communication is very important as it will help the decision-maker know the premise or context to tailor-make the decisions. Bureaucratic communication channels are used to choke the flow of information on both ends, leading to faulty decision-making. Similarly, the communication from the decision-makers should be informative, and it must follow a proper channel of percolation to the bottom end. The channel selection for propagating the decisions in today's world can be one of the toughest challenges. Therefore, communicating decisions through social networks may not be so effective for employees who are working mostly under dust or fumes or in standing postures. Maybe that is why ***Facebook workplace***[53] is not so successful at the shop floor level, but it is a good communication channel capable for a higher impact in internal communication in IT organizations where most employees and stakeholders are technically hyperactive.

#### 4.3.2. Second C – Competence

The tussle between the *Fuehrer Hitler* and *Erwin Rommel* was due to a perception of competence. The answer, according to history, was 'Yes'.

While nurturing raw talent, leaders often underestimate the chances that the follower can surpass the leader and demonstrate in the practical field. Rommel surpassed Hitler in the competence of leadership, camaraderie[54], and knowledge of warfare. Most probably, due to this reason, Hitler gradually perceived Rommel as a potential competitor or a threat rather than a talent with immense potential. On the other hand, Rommel understood that he had the talent and tried to supersede the instructions. As a result, the lack of support and coordination during the tough times came into existence, which confused the German army, and they ultimately became defunct.

The same situation is prevailing in the corporate world. The perception of competence between the decision-maker and the decision-taker varies significantly. As a result, talented decision-takers may be viewed as potential threats and side-lined by being put into projects of least importance or assignments where decisions are mundane. Decision-makers must encourage the line management to be associated with decisions of importance so that the passing of bucks can be replaced by owning the decisions even in case of failure.

Senior leadership is always judged by its ability to coordinate, which can be in terms of hiring the top brass who can have the vision to achieve the goals of the organization through collaborative efforts. Secondly, it must understand issues of line management and, based on the same, formulate decisions that can appropriately cater to both organizational vision and mission statements. Lastly, every decision must have transparency and a guided plan of action; otherwise, it will never accord the desired acceptance from the wider business population.

### 4.3.3. Third C – Credibility

In the anecdote, it is clearly evidenced that there was a clear disconnection of credibility at the decision-maker's end. The selection and nurturing of *Erwin Rommel* was no doubt an act of credibility for *Hitler* as he was well-accepted as a leader of the German army and one of the few German generals who were equally accepted by the enemies as well. However, during the early 1940s, Hitler showed stepmotherly behavior to Rommel due to his popularity and control over the army. Credibility is a two-way traffic and is based on trust that a leader must demonstrate. Unfortunately, trust was missing between the two and, therefore, Hitler lost his credibility in the eyes of Rommel.

The responsibility of decision-making stakeholders is not limited to hiring and nurturing leaders with a vision and belief system in sync with the organization; it is equally important for the organization to indoctrinate the leaders by harnessing two-way communication and creating a transparent culture with a local leadership team. Credible leaders always focus on talent inclusivity and churning out talents, which, in turn, provides ample opportunities for home-grown talents to flourish.

## *4.4. Conclusion*

According to figure I of 3C framework, the intersection of Communication, Competence and Credibility can be considered an ideal decision which is implementable and effective for the organization. However, eminent readers must have observed that it is a small cross-section of the whole area, which clearly points out the fact that very few decisions of decision-makers are unchallenged at the operational level because the relevance of all the 3Cs is necessary for any decision to sustain and pass the test of time to generate desired result across the organization for better today and tomorrow.

# Chapter| 5

## Effective Reward & Recognition Programs – Overcoming the Dilemma of Role Importance vs. Person Visibility

### *5.1. Introduction*

It is a well-admitted fact that sound reward and recognition programs can have a far-reaching impact and positive correlation on employee engagement and retention across hierarchies in any organization. In order to enjoy a cutting edge over their competitors, organizations keep on revisiting their existing R&R (Reward & Recognition)[55] programs and, at the same time, devising new programs that can effectively enhance employee engagement and at the same time, can be used as a tool for employee retention.

Unfortunately, despite all the diligence in designing and administering, most of such R&R programs slowly become mere formality or are accused of a high level of subjectivity ***(one of my colleagues correctly named it "Case-to-Case – Face-to-Face").*** Most of the time, HR managers are blamed for taking part in these exercises without judging the relative merit that ultimately culminates into ***Case-to-Case – Face-to-Face*** or subjective decisions.

Let us make a deep stick investigation to figure out the possible causes that can make any R&R initiatives a counterproductive one.

### *5.2. Case to Case – Face to Face – What Is It?*

As HR managers, most of us are accustomed to the above, but we avoid exceptions and subjectivity very delicately.

Let us try to examine how the reward and recognition policies vary based on two broad variables, namely:

- **Role Importance**
- **Person Visibility**

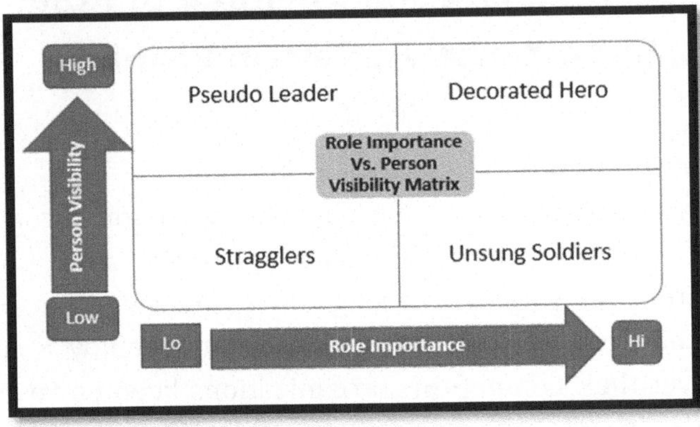


*Figure 5.1*

Let us have a journey through the above 2 X 2 matrix in which all the quadrants are labelled against their degree (High or Low) with respect to role importance (RI) and person visibility (PV). Objectives of rewards and recognition programs for all four levels are different in nature.

***Scenario I – High RI & High PV*** – Such a person can be labeled as a ***'Decorated Hero'*** for any organization. Most of the people in leadership positions or aspiring leaders are located in such a quadrant. The majority of the organizations are pampering their ***'Heroes'*** to keep them engaged and motivated by using the following R&R interventions.

**The objective of the R&R Program: Sustenance of motivation, enhanced engagement, and resultant retention of 'Decorated Heroes'.**

- Both intrinsic as well as extrinsic motivation[56]

- Faster career growth and constituent reward and recognition
- Use of retention bonus plan and stock options as a tool to increase their overall compensation package.
- Promoting their organizational recognition, which, in turn, reinforces their societal recognition and acceptance.
- Continued scope for interaction with senior management to enrich their knowledge base and, at the same time, enhance their visibilities, which act as a deciding factor in deciding the type and quantum of R&R

***Scenario II - High RI & Low PV*** - It can be presumed that most HR professionals have come across ***'Unsung Soldiers'*** with high role importance but low (or lack of) person visibility. Unfortunately, such employees constitute the largest chunk fitted in the Bell Curve. Organizations, nowadays, hardly bother with their retention, but the pathetic truth is attrition in sizable numbers of ***'Unsung Heroes'*** weakens the bottom line of operation in any organization, be they are sales executives of an FMCG sector or site engineers of a project organization or maybe shift officers of a press shop unit of a factory. Most organizations adopt the following R&R measures mainly focused on maintaining a minimum level of motivation.

**The objective of the R&R Program: The focus is mainly on intrinsic motivation[57] and minimum engagement and retention of 'Unsung Soldiers.'**

- Mostly, verbal praise or appreciation is used to boost motivation superficially.
- Only average reward administration coupled with low to moderate career progression[58].

- Reward and recognition programs are used on a piecemeal basis rather than structured intervention.
- Training is used as a retention tool rather than honing competencies.
- Restricted developmental initiative for equipping *'Unsung Soldiers'* for long-term employability.

***Scenario III - Low RI & Low PV*** – Most organizations have people holding the position of ***'Stragglers'*** with low role importance and person visibility. Think about the positions of a data entry operator or computer hardware assistant discharging mundane types of operations day in and day out. To find out whether the organizations are serious enough to hone their competencies or not, R&R programs are meant to be focused on these target audiences. Due to a lack of developmental opportunities coupled with low recognition, such a chunk of staff can suffer from **'Low self-esteem[59]'** and feelings of obsolescence. Such employees commonly fall under the category of 'Actively Disengaged Employees'.

***Scenario IV - Low RI & High PV*** – In our day-to-day work operation, we come across a variety of employees in the form of bosses, co-workers, and junior colleagues may be in all three categories depicted above. However, have you ever seen people who like to draw the attention of others and poke their noses into the operation of others or appease the leaders to manipulate resources and career opportunities? Despite their low role importance, they easily catch the attention of others. It may be for this reason that some of these positions enjoy more authority than an *'Unsung Soldier.'* That is the reason these categories of employees are called ***'Pseudo Leaders.'***
**The objective of the R&R Program: The focus is mainly on extrinsic motivation, high engagement, and retention.**

- Reward and recognition are entirely based on ***Face-to-Face*** basis. The degree of person visibility decides the degree and quantum of rewards and recognition.
- Recognition in the form of safeguarding their roles by switching from a lower-importance role to a higher one (the terminology of job enlargement or enrichment is not ideally applicable here). (Maybe due to this reason, in the last decade, front office executives or receptionists (of course, the capability of pseudo leadership) were re-designated or refitted as administration executives or even absorbed in the HR department based on their degree of PV (Person Visibility).
- Training is used as a tool to equip them just to swim with the people with high role importance named ***'Unsung Soldiers.'***
- Talent management programs are selectively used for these sets of employees to upgrade them to the first quadrant of ***'Decorated Heroes'.***

To overcome this dilemma, the organization can devise and deliver R&R policies with the following essential ingredients:

- Reward and recognition policies must be based on objectively set criteria.
- They should maintain immediacy.
- They should focus specifically on the ***'Decorated Heroes'*** who are going to affect the top end of the organization.
- They must properly address the requirement of the ***'Unsung Soldiers'*** whose sustained contribution affects the bottom end of the organization. The contribution of such soldiers cannot be overlooked, as

no one knows when they will glitter and shine like a hero.

- R&R programs must not promote a climate of appeasement or a channel to protect some cross-section of employees facing obsolesces. Adequate precaution must be adopted to deal with ***Pseudo-Leaders.***
- '***Stragglers***' should also be covered under R&R policies to boost their morale, which can, in turn, ramify into a greater contribution to organizational success.
- R&R programs must not fall in the net of ***Case-to-Case (Role Specific***) or ***Face-to-Face (Position Specific).***

In a nutshell, it can be concluded that '***Creating credibility is everyone's responsibility,***' and it is good for any reward and recognition program to reap the desired success.

# Chapter| 6

## Power of Empathy: Mastering Interpersonal Effectiveness

*We can't practise empathy if we don't believe people. The quickest path to an empathic miss and disconnection is to evaluate and judge what people are sharing with us through the lens of our lived experiences, rather than listening plus believing.*

***– Brené Brown in the Twitter***

*6.1. Foreword*

One of the common skills for successful interpersonal effectiveness for any manager is empathy[60]. Usually, it is expressed by putting the others' shoes on your feet and judging them. But how frequently it is practised and/or on how many such occasions someone practises it remains a million-dollar question. Nevertheless, empathy will always remain a well-promulgated yet neglected behavioural attribute.

The chapter aims to understand the definition of empathy and its interconnections with interpersonal effectiveness.

Also, efforts will be made so that the budding talents of tomorrow can understand the impact of empathy on human relations in the workplace. In the next section, we will try to figure out the difference between sympathy[61] and empathy because, though both are seemingly different, most of the time, they are misunderstood, and as a result, instead of empathy, the former takes the front seats. As the author of the book, I am sure that after going through the chapter, budding professionals will acquire some ideas on empathy to practise in everyday life.

*6.2. Empathy vs. Sympathy – Concept and Context*

Let me take the opportunity to ask ourselves: What type of reactions or emotions does someone have while conveying the news of a close colleague's accident to their kith and kin and conveying the same news to the parents of their servant who encountered an accident? Will the intensity of emotions remain the same in both incidents?

Just pull back for two minutes and think patiently to understand your emotions associated with two different types of episodes. If the emotions are different in two separate cases, please spare a few more minutes to deep-dive and try to differentiate the two distinctive emotions emanating from the mind. Initially, it seems to be considerably tough to differentiate the two emotions termed ***'Empathy'*** and ***'Sympathy'*** as both are inextricably intertwined.

The illustrations may have thrown some light on the context of the chapter. Therefore, it is now high time to move towards the definition of the words *Sympathy* and *Empathy*, which will surely uncover a few more attributes.

According to Hodges and Myers in the book *Social Psychology*, *Empathy* is defined as understanding someone else's experience by imagining yourself in that person's situation. Therefore, the definition suggests that there is an immense necessity for an emotional connection to feel someone else's feelings and respond appropriately without being judgemental. On the other hand, *Sympathy* is defined as understanding someone else's suffering or sadness. One thing that is distinctively clear is that empathy connect with the person, cognition of incidence and identification with the person and incidence all are interconnected and act as an agent for empathy to occur. On the contrary, sympathy, cognition and concern act as integrating factors. Sympathy literally means *'feeling with,'* while empathy means *'feeling into.'*

### *6.3. Empathy in the Workplace – Walking an Extra Mile*

In an organization, particularly in the field of human resources, it is being widely propagated by the HR leaders to be empathetic towards internal customers who are employees and also external customers. One of the principal reasons is that in any organization, both people and processes are interconnected, and these interfaces can evoke confusion, frustration, and grievance, which can only be addressed through proper empathy and subsequent response. On many occasions, people-to-people communication creates frustration, agitation and grievance, while in an organization with a high degree of technological readiness, emotional disruptions remain unaddressed, and when they surface, neither the immediate boss nor the human resource representative can recover the damage.

Unfortunately, in an organization, this essential attribute is often overlooked, mixed up with sympathy and judgment, and culminates in emotional discontentment. Eminent readers may wonder what causes this disruption in empathy when most of the professionals have the requisite qualifications and experience. Let us try to unravel those hindering factors preventing empathy from growing with flying colours.

- ***Lack of Listening Skill*** – In today's corporate world, almost everyone would like to be a speaker and ample training programs are designed to develop a speaker. It is true that good speaking skills can be a game changer in most cases while bagging big contracts or presenting a newly launched product. But, there is hardly anyone who comes across a training program to develop their effective listening skills, and even if it is designed, it is not going to be a choice of the target audience. Due to a lack of sincere and patient listening skills, the germination of empathy becomes limited and most probably restricted to close workgroups with similar beliefs and thoughts.

- ***Judgemental*** – People generally tend to judge the whole incidence based on the initial sets of information, which is also called ***Anchoring Bias***[62]. This can act as a hindrance to empathy and create a disconnect. Sometimes, people become too judgmental due to ***Availability Bias***[63], which is defined as a tendency to think that examples of things that come readily to mind are more representative than the actual case. This creates a propensity to judge any incidence in the light of personal experience of a somewhat similar kind. Due to availability bias, when we come across the news of a car accident committed by a reputed actor, we draw a quick conclusion of reckless driving, but when the same incident happens to a colleague or a classmate, we judge it as a fault of the pedestrian.
- ***Mutual Trust and Respect*** – Empathy is a two-way process of sharing thoughts and experiences. It involves active listening and internalizing the facts without being judgemental. Therefore, mutual respect and rapport are absolutely mandatory; you have to believe first and then respond in an empathetic way to the other. Unfortunately, in today's organizations, mutual trust and respect, in a true sense, are rare to locate; hence, the empathetic response from one end to the other is also rare. In most cases, empathy is used as a tool to cool down the grievance of employees as a part of mundane

employee connect with the associated performance index to capture the efficacy of HR functions.

- ***Egocentrism*[64]** – It refers to someone's inability to understand and appreciate others' views or feelings different from their own. Egocentrism is a ***cognitive bias*[65]** in which someone assumes that others share the same perspective as they do and cannot have a perception of their own. Any empathy dialogue majorly fails in the ice-breaking process itself due to the possible egocentrism of either or both parties involved in the process.
- ***Lack of Interest*** – Another sad part of empathic miss is the lack of interest in human relations. On several occasions, showing empathy can be confused with counselling and can end up being a one-way communication with a few readymade panaceas for improving mental and occupational health. It is also a fact that most people, whether in HR or Head of Units, treat it as add-on work without any benefits.
- ***Underestimation of Context*** – By this time, it is quite clear to all the readers that empathy is always preferred to be a spontaneous act of compassion, and it has to be imbibed into the belief system of the individuals. However, contextual or circumstantial settings are also equally important for empathy to generate a visible result. It is not at all prudent to show empathy to an employee who has just come to know that his promotion has been dropped for the year. Empathetic discussion without due consideration of context often leads to a 'wishy-washy' outcome.
- ***Individual Credibility*** – Last but not least, the credibility of an individual can always walk an extra mile in the journey of empathy. The moment an individual feels that

the facts and experiences are collected by the other side with a hidden agenda of cross-verification or mere extraction of information for the official purpose, the credibility goes off and becomes hard to regain under any circumstances. It is quite pertinent that the empathizer should be credible enough to do justice to their role by creating an environment of mutual understanding and rapport under which the whole process can be completed.

### *6.4. Empathy with Emotional Connect – Developing Empathy Matrix*

To better understand and appreciate the process of empathy, it is now high time to relate it to emotional connect. Based on the conceptual understanding of *empathy*, in this section, an effort will be made to create an ***'Empathy Matrix'*** to derive variance in empathy in four distinct situations. A note of disclaimer can be noted forthwith that the designing of the matrix is based on individual perception and more than two decades of experience in the field of human resources.

Based on the ***2 X 2 Empathy Matrix***, an attempt will be made to figure out the right fit for the personal and professional life. Also, the framework will try to provide the direction in which flow empathy is desirable or not so desirable. ***Degree of Emotional Connect*** (***connoted as DoEC***) will be taken as an independent variable and ***Degree of Empathy*** (***connoted as DoE***) will be taken as a dependent variable. Both the variables can be either 'High' or 'Low'.

Let us now examine in detail the four distinct situations and the resultant degree of empathy.

- ***Situation A – High DoEC and High DoE*** – The individuals who fall into this category can be termed ***'Empathic Healers.'*** Due to the high emotional connect with people, these individuals can easily identify, visualize and summarize the pain points of others. As the name suggests, people with such a capability generally also have a rich life experience that they can utilize effectively in the process of empathy and conclude the process with a possible set of solutions. *That may be a possible reason why childhood buddies are perceived to possess a high degree of emotional connect, and therefore, top-secret information can be shared with them.*

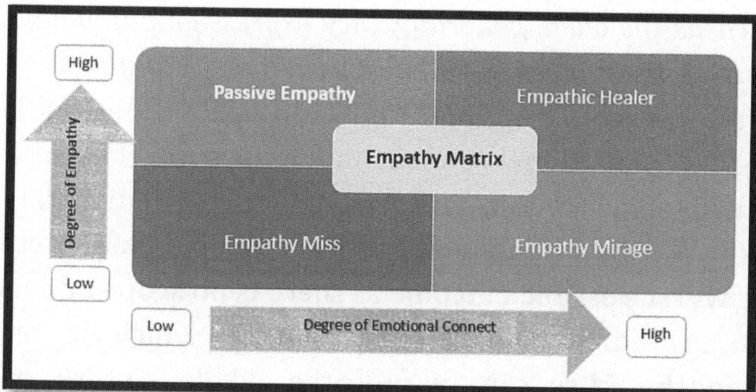


*Figure 6.1*

- ***Situation B - High DoEC and Low DoE*** – Can anyone think of a situation where they share some sensitive pain areas with someone who apparently seems to be empathetic? However, it is actually the opposite. Due to this, the situation is termed ***'Empathy Mirage.'*** Individuals with a high level of emotional connect but low empathy can damage the process of empathy by creating a veil. *Most of the grapevine discussions and workplace gossips are originated from initial discussions in which individuals can be trapped in the mirage of empathy and end up sharing vital personal information.*
- ***Situation C – Low DoEC and High DoE*** – Task-centric bosses often ignore the value of emotional connectivity

with junior colleagues despite their high degree of empathy. According to these individuals, a high-level emotional connect may affect the business deliverables or they may be perceived to be taken for granted. As a result, such individuals can passively express their empathy ***(Passive Empathy).*** *In everyday life, you can visualise this situation well. In the parent-child interaction, fathers generally maintain lower emotional connect and are considered to be strict, but due to a high degree of empathy towards the child, generally, they express empathy passively through the mother. It can also be termed* ***'Tough Love.'***

- ***Situation D – Low DoEC and Low DoE*** **–** Due to a lower degree of emotional connect, individuals may lack or avoid sensitive discussion, and the only thing individuals are doing is 'Mind your own business.' This situation creates the worst possible outcome as there is no scope or concern for an individual. Such a situation, which is termed ***'Empathy Miss,'*** can disrupt the whole culture of the organization and can create a high amount of emotional burnout, which, in the long run, may result in lower self-esteem. In *traditionally managed family-run organizations, due to this low level of emotional connect and low level of empathy, people are often accustomed to work despite harsh words. The possible reason may be that people are just trying to survive due to repeated emotional burnouts but do not have any self-esteem for survival.*

The word *Empathy* aptly suggests putting the shoes of others on your feet, but actually, it can have much more ramifications in honing and nurturing even the official relationship. It is not just a mere one-shot affair; rather, it is a process that initiates with gaining mutual trust by bridging the emotional gap and is finally completed with a response of a lifetime. Every single incidence of empathetic interaction can itself leverage the inner power of empathy within us, and every single incident we come across from our colleagues, juniors, superiors, or any other can be stored as an empathy repository in our conscious mind and can be retrieved and visualized when it is required. Empathy is not how one feels but how you feel if you were in that position. If it is visualized properly with internalization, then only the power of empathy can be exerted meaningfully.

# Chapter| 7

## Understanding and Designing Goal Setting Process Using LEARN Framework

### *7.1. Foreword*

The chapter aims to understand the impact of the pandemic on the overall socio-economy, and based on the set premise, efforts will be made to recommend a supportive framework for the setting of goals for entry-level employees and new recruits as most of them are now and will be operating from home, which is commonly termed *WFH (Work From Home),* maybe for another year.

The traditional goal-setting processes may not be a suitable or acceptable option to capture the performance of newcomers during the post-COVID era of new normal life. However, before suggesting the framework, it is imperative to understand the impact of the pandemic on business, the supply-and-demand crisis and its impact on employee performance, specifically fresh recruits from campuses. Despite the dull business scenario, most organizations hired from campuses and completed on-boarding processes through virtual platforms by the end of July.

### *7.2. The Cycle of Business Downturn*

The entire globe was under the grip of the pandemic posed by SARS-COVID-2 *alias* Corona; however, we felt the heat only when the nationwide lockdown was announced by the Ministry of Home Affairs at the end of March of the last financial year of 2019-2020. During that period, we saw how the Indian and the global economy melted down and industries, irrespective of their size, nature, and product, suffered an unprecedented and somewhat irrecoverable jolt.

Due to the total global lockdown, service sectors like Airlines, Tourism and Hospitality, Retail and Reality were almost on the brink of terminal collapse, resulting in a huge loss of employment and prospective employment opportunities. Overall, business disruption can be categorized into six distinct stages, ultimately pushing the economy into the cycle of business downturn. Let us ponder this aspect through a diagrammatic view.

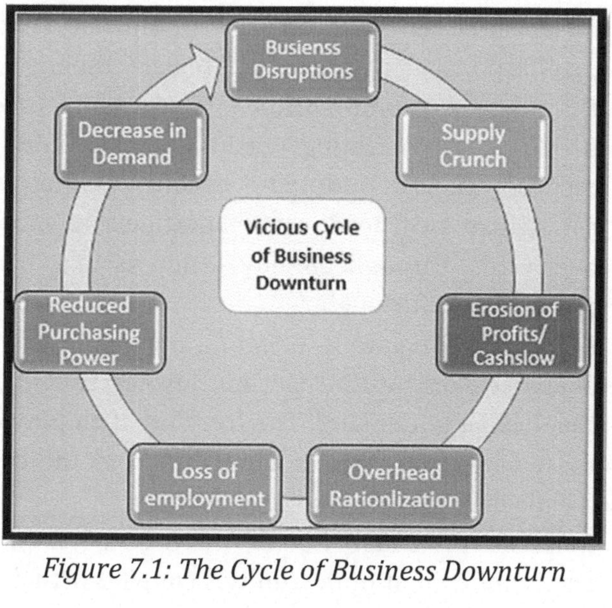


*Figure 7.1: The Cycle of Business Downturn*

1. ***Business Disruptions*** – Due to the initial surge in COVID cases across the globe, particularly in the US and other Western European countries, there was a slowing down and temporary to permanent closure of business or manufacturing activities.

2. ***Supply Crunch*** – During the first lockdown, the tendency to hoard significantly increased, particularly in the household sector, which temporarily created a pseudo-increase in demand. However, due to the suspension of manufacturing processes and other business activities, a supply crunch or shortage was evident, which resulted in improperly higher pricing.
3. ***Erosion of Profits/ Cash Flow*** – Profit erosion is mainly caused by supply crunch and rapid decline in household purchasing power predominantly due to loss of employment or fear of the same. One of the major difficulties faced by all organizations, irrespective of their size, is significant erosion of profits, particularly from April to September.
4. ***Overhead Rationalization*** – To respond to eroded profits and declining cash flows, major Indian incorporations adopted drastic initiatives to rationalize overhead cost[66], particularly manpower overheads, through employee downsizing, benching, pay cuts, and furloughs.
5. ***Loss of Employment*** – Significant employment loss, evidenced during this period, further contributed to the decline in demand. The freezing of employment in most organizations also contributed to the declining trends in employment opportunities.
6. ***Reduced Purchase Power***[67] – Loss of employment and employment opportunities coupled with declining purchasing power of the household sector culminated in a decline in demand. Such a cyclical business pattern resulted in *'The Cycle of Business Downturn.'* Every organization tries to move out of it to ensure business continuity.

### *7.3. A Few Words on Business Continuity*

During the initial phase of the series of lockdowns, the predominant challenge for any organization was to maintain the wellness and engagement levels of employees despite the bleak atmosphere of business. Organizations, based on the criticality of the operation, adopted cautious approaches to ensure business continuity. Most of the popularized and well-accepted approaches for business continuity during the series of lockdowns were working remotely based on the nature of jobs. It not only helped organizations save fixed overheads and capital expenditure but also safeguarded the health and hygiene of the workforce associated with the industry.

As a result, various austerity measures, training, and development activities were restricted to virtual mode, and this continued for at least the following year, if not more. Substantial emphasis was put on digital initiatives to reduce manpower involvement, particularly in the field of work scheduling and monitoring. A survey report by PwC conducted on 60 executives in late April 2020 has shown that 60% of executives expressed their opinion in favour of making remote working permanent, and 17% opined in favour of Furlough.

It is also worth mentioning that due to a sharp surge in e-commerce[68] business, employment generation in the gig economy[69] increased quite exponentially, and major players in these sectors shifted their focus to India as a hub for such activities.

### *7.4. Practical Challenges in Goal-Setting – Remedial Measures*

Amidst the pandemic and the concern for business continuity, most of the reputed organizations advocated for the performance appraisal processes as per the schedule, despite the fact that the result might depend on profitability and cash flows from the business. However, the following problems may potentially hinder the goal-setting processes for employees with less experience:

- During most of this calendar year, resources are idle due to the pandemic and consequent business downturn. Hence, traditional KRA/KPI facts and figures may not provide a clear understanding of the setting of ***SMART***[70] goals. Even though the lockdowns have been lifted, sustained business outcomes are doubtful due to various socio-economic issues and mitigation of the pandemic.
- Secondly, after getting accustomed to working from remote locations due to social distancing practices prescribed in various advisories, it is becoming tough for both juniors and superiors to interact face-to-face and discuss the process of goal setting. In Indian culture, more importance is given to direct interactions than to virtual ones. Therefore, the goal-setting processes on traditional parameters without considering potentials can be detrimental to the process and people.
- Thirdly, comparatively junior employees with less than three years of experience or maybe the newly inducted fresh campus recruits possess certain levels of career aspirations from the organizations in respect of learning and development, growth plan and recognition. At the same time, organizations also have expectations, particularly with respect to agility and adaptability to the new normal work culture, digital adaptability, customer focus and out-of-the-box thinking. To understand and appreciate the two-way dynamics, it is very pertinent to suggest a framework that can balance mutual expectations.

- Fourthly, the majority of organizations, due to overhead reduction, are walking on the path of pay cuts and withholding of increments; under such a scenario, instilling morale in **Gen Y** or **Gen Z** (generation cohorts[71]) is very important to keep the hope alive by devising appropriate performance criterion by which goal-setting processes can be initiated. The performance standard should be suitable enough to capture the potentiality in addition to hard-core quantifiable figures, which are themselves dismal due to the business downturn. Also, efforts should be made to integrate the suggested performance dimensions with the traditional ***SMART*** goals to make them objective and robust.

Since most of the downsizing and furloughs are initiated based on performance scores, traditional goal dimensions can prove to be counterproductive. Such a fear factor among employees may create a negative impression about goal-setting and appraisal processes across organizations. Hence, traditional dimensions can be viewed as a punitive tool or a premise for punitive action.

This may be the ideal time for organizations to objectively explore talent assessment and mapping by designing an effective framework that can sustainably focus on employee potentiality. Such a framework can also delve into a structured process through which some of the key business aspects have become more important to achieving individual and organizational goals.

Finally, setting goals based on ***LEARN*** framework makes the performance conversation much more developmental and constructive since the framework itself takes care of developmental dimensions and is integrated with ***SMART*** goals to get a unique blend of outcomes that can balance the expectations of the immediate superior and the job holder.

*7.5. The Elements of LEARN Framework: A Discussion*

I hope, by this time, eminent readers have already understood that effort is being made to suggest dimensions with which goal-setting exercise can be done by the following *SMART* approach (***Specific, Measurable, Achievable, Relevant and Time-Bound).*** Similarly, our suggested framework, known as ***LEARN***, also has five unique performance ingredients that can take care of both qualitative and quantitative dimensions. Also, it is strongly *in sync* with the widely used goal-setting process mentioned above. Let us travel through each ingredient of the framework.

- ***L – Learning Agility to Integrate Theoretical Knowledge into the Practical Field:*** After the pandemic, when the lockdowns were lifted, disruptive changes occurred in the workplace, which are relevant even to the new normal life. However, the centre stone will be the pace of learning as organizations are striving to achieve quick and immediate results to minimize the losses in revenues during business disruptions. So, the future will be secure for those who are part of the agile workforce and are always ready to learn and implement with greater ease by assimilating theory into practice. Sometimes, the process of learning and implementation takes some time, but such a dimension must be captured in an organization repository. Also, it helps understand the skills already developed and the skills that require developmental action.
- ***E – Enthusiasm for Customer Delight (Internal & External):*** Post- pandemic, a new normal workplace

was characterized by many disruptive changes, including more involvement of digital technology for process monitoring and minutely detecting the deviation from the planned activities. Lesser human interference in the core operational process will be the need of the day. Hence, human resources can be leveraged for customer delight, be it internal or external stakeholders. Importance will be given to those who are keenly enthusiastic to serve the customers and enjoy interacting to ensure customer delight and simultaneously enhance effective networking.

- ***A – Acumen for Business and Quality Consciousness***: Ensuring resource optimization in every sphere of the operation of any industry is the need of the hour. This can only be possible by allocating the right quality and quantity of resources at the right time and at the right operation with minimal wastage, greater quality and fewer rejections or rework. The whole essence of business processes during the unlocking time will be the judicious deployment of resources with greater productivity. Hence, employees at the junior level or trainees from campuses must have the acumen or fair knowledge of business excellence to act actively as business partners.
- ***R – Receptivity in Accepting Process Changes:*** The new normal work life is going through a lot of disruptions and drastic changes. The changes are dramatic and can replace the existing systems with redundant ones. Organizations have expectations from newcomers regarding digital adoption and process changes. It is needless to mention that one of the probable reasons for continuing campus hiring

amidst the pandemic was to groom future leaders who can readily embrace digitalization.

- ***N - Novelty of Thinking and Ideation:*** Lastly, continuous innovation and changes are becoming the mantra for business sustenance. Maybe due to this, we have seen players who used to manufacture products like soaps, detergents, and even non-essential products have started manufacturing hygiene products like masks, sanitizers, etc. Henceforth, novelty or out-of-the-box thinking will be an ingredient that every organization is going to nurture for business sustenance. During the lockdowns, many ideation processes were widely used by the organizations regarding process control, analytics and process improvement. Therefore, many expect junior employees and campus trainees to contribute in these areas for better business sustenance and improvement in the quality of talents deployed.

### *7.6. Integration of LEARN Framework with SMART Goal-Setting – A Sample Illustration*

LEARN framework is a standalone system that can work in isolation. However, it can neutralize the negative mindset of employees, especially junior and fresh recruits who are going through a tough time. The suggested system can leverage and highlight certain factors that will have a greater probability of understanding the talent. The framework can make the goal-setting process more robust by bridging the gap between the expectations of the employees and the expectations of the employer. Let us follow ***Table No I of 5 X 5 Matrix,*** where the author has tried to figure out the interface of ***SMART*** with ***LEARN*** for a sample goal-setting framework and setting the context of two processes to operate in tandem.

| Sample SMART Goals and LEARN performance dimensions interface for Jr. Executive – HR/ Trainee HR | | | | | |
|---|---|---|---|---|---|
| | S – Specific | M - Measurable | A - Achievable | R - Relevant | T- Time bound |
| L – Learning Agility | Understanding of Success Factors<br><br>Implementation of My Zone Success factors | Number of awareness workshop attended<br><br>% of data migrated from old HRMS system | Post training Assessment score >=90%<br><br>>= 95% data to be migrated time | Critical and Relevant for Role | Within 31.12.2020 |
| E -Enthusiasm for customer delight (internal & external) | Coordination with HODs for on time appraisal feedback<br><br>Completion of Employee Satisfaction Survey | Number of Sessions planned Vs Actual<br><br>Survey planned Vs Implemented | >= 80%<br><br>Avg. Satisfaction index >= 85% | Critical and Relevant for Role | 100% completion by 31.03.2020 |
| A – Acumen for business and quality consciousness | Staff Productivity<br><br>Manpower Cost as % revenue | Revenue/Employee<br><br>Return on Talent Employed (ROTE) on PBIT | Planned Vs. Actual Achievement | Critical and Relevant for Role | Monthly Productivity vs Staff count |
| R -Receptivity in accepting process changes | Updating of Employee Skill Inventory in Success Factors | Understanding of system through hands on training<br><br>Number of follow up planned Vs. Actual follow up | Post Training Assessment Score >= 95%<br><br>>= 90% | Critical and Relevant for Role | Skill Mapping completion by 31.12.2020 |
| N – Novelty of thinking & ideation | Ideation of at least one Unique employee engagement initiative per 6 months.<br><br>Ideation for one such actionable process improvement suggestion / year | Actual number of man days spend on ideation/ design/ presentation and implementation | >= 2.0 such unique activities<br><br>>= 1.0 such actionable suggestion | Critical and Relevant for Role | Midterm review 30.06.2020<br><br>Yearly Appraisal |

*Table 7.1: Goal Setting – Using SMART/ LEARN Framework*

### *7.7. Concluding Comments*

Throughout the chapter, an attempt was made to raise awareness of the disruptive changes. Solid foundational input was provided to all eminent readers so that they could accept the situation and its challenges and possibilities so that various business decisions could be aligned with changing scenarios.

Human Resources are no exception and cannot function in silos. Therefore, introducing the developmental dimension into goal-setting processes is imperative in the changed workplace scenario. With this objective in mind, an alternative framework called ***LEARN*** has been designed, which will surely be reviewed in parallel and integrated with ***SMART*** goal-setting process to make the whole goal-setting exercise more robust and relevant for the present scenario. However, it is always recommended to consider the framework as a supportive tool rather than a standalone framework to ensure its efficacy; also, at the same time, actionable and validated quantifiable data must be kept handy for effective usage of the framework. Lastly, the write-up concludes with a disclaimer stating that the framework offered never claimed to be a sacrosanct one and that it is purely based on the experience and expertise of the author of the topic of discussion.

# Chapter| 8

## Three Yoga Sutras of the Bhagavad Gita: A Source toward the Improvement of HR Functions

*8.1. Gliding through the Changes*

Corporate life after the pandemic has undergone a huge paradigm shift and continuous socio-technological disruptions, ramifying the changes in the pattern of interfaces between people and people-driven processes. These disruptions are not only restricted to the people and processes but also encompass the relationship between the organization and the individual. The traditional mode of face-to-face communication has been replaced by virtual communication using AI platforms, which, on the one hand, makes communication easier but, on the other hand, makes connecting harder. Across the globe, there has been a huge change in the pattern of communication in upward, downward, horizontal, and diagonal directions; hence, managing expectations has become more complex and subject to subjectivity.

Mitigating the communication gap has become a crucial agenda for all CHRO (*Chief Human Resource Officer*) across the business, irrespective of the size of the organization or the type of business. Therefore, it is becoming pertinent for all leaders to connect meaningfully with their direct reports and peers with higher emotional intelligence to minimize communication distortions.

### *8.2. Business Transformation and Reality at Ground Zero*

After the lockdowns were lifted, organizations began widely practising a few systems like Work from Home, remote working, and gig working. Due to this reason, nowadays, employment insertions specify the typology of employment as on-site or remote working, which has already changed and probably would change further with the span of time.

In addition, rapid digitalization and widespread usage of Artificial Intelligence coupled with drone technology paved the way for *Industrial Revolution 4.0*[72]. It is a well-accepted fact that today's businesses are focusing more on the accuracy of the outcome measurement rather than chasing blindfolded business forecasts.

However, a question that is still unanswered is whether the beneficiaries of the Industrial Revolution 4.0 are solely the organizations or the employees are equally benefitted. Perhaps work practices, namely Work from Home (WFH), opened the door of *Work from Home and Work for Home,* which is indicative of balancing work and life. There is a growing demand, particularly from Gen Z, to balance their work and personal lives and meaningful roles, which can add value to their professional growth. Employee wellness during the post-pandemic period played a crucial role in the discussion point as it is the toughest job of all to synchronize the wiring of the heart and mind of any human being to derive performance on a sustained basis.

It is becoming increasingly challenging for human resources professionals to leverage talent towards business excellence coupled with retaining the talent pool by engaging them in the role with learning and growth opportunities.

### *8.3. The Hidden Factors Are the Key Factors*

By now, the readers must have understood that developing talents through appropriate developmental interventions and managing talents through performance monitoring and feedback can act as a double-edged sword because potential performers, unless satisfied with the organizational culture and career progression, can step out, leaving behind a vacuum with huge recruitment costs.

It is a formidable challenge to retain talents across businesses, and despite all efforts to discuss retention, there is a significant exodus of skilled manpower in every industry. So, what are those hidden factors that keep the talents in an organization for a longer period of time and help them contribute toward business success? Though they are occasionally overlooked, perhaps it is not a daunting task to identify those hidden factors, and retention strategy remains at the center of discussion at any conference of human resources.

In the next section, some exploration will be made using the principles of *The Bhagavad Gita,* a holy book that is a rich source of harmonizing the heart and mind to unleash human potential. In the world of business uncertainty, a few of Lord Krishna's preachings, which helped Arjuna unleash his full potential during the war of Kurukshetra, can improve people-to-people connections by using the concept of *Karma.*

*The Bhagavad Geeta*[73] *– devising for the better people connection*

Therefore, every HR professional is barraged with assignments; most of them are mundane but important for organizational sustenance, while a few others are firefighting. Some of these tasks also have short to medium-term strategic importance.

However, one element of Human Resources Management that is common across organizations is managing Human Relations at a workplace, which consists of managing individual expectations, emotions, aspirations, and dreams. Based on this context, apart from sound domain knowledge, every HR professional must have the following:

- A sound customer orientation and operational focus to cater efficiently to the needs of internal and external customers and stakeholders.
- Empathy to understand and connect with people to build up a relationship of mutual trust and harmony at the workplace.
- Patience to accept and appreciate differences and handle situations in a humane way.

All the above attributes are well-taught in B-schools or organizations during the socialization processes of an HR professional. However, it is a less-known fact that all these guidelines were highlighted in metaphors thousands of years ago in The Gita's 3 Yoga sutras, namely: Karma, Bhakti, and Gyana Yoga. Let us try to unearth those metaphors below through a diagrammatic viewpoint.

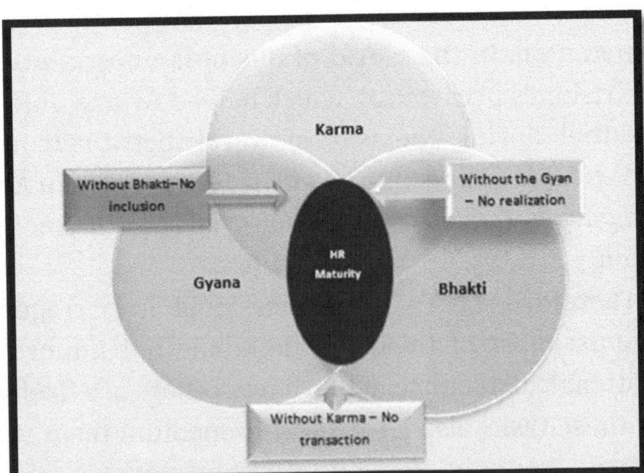


*Figure 8.1*

*Source: My Gita by Devdutta Pattanaik*

- **Karma Yoga**

*Karma yoga* is one of the four classical schools of yoga alongside *Jnana* (knowledge or self-study), *Bhakti* (devotion), and *Raja* (meditation), each offering a path to *moksha* (spiritual liberation) and self-realization.

Derived from the Sanskrit term for ***"action,"*** *karma* is understood by both Hindu and Buddhist traditions to be the sum of a person's deeds in past, present, and future states of existence. It entails the outcome of every action, good or bad, right or wrong, depending on the kind of action one takes.

In yoga, *karma* is known as the path of action or selfless service towards others. (Source: *https://www. yogapedia. com/*). The word *Karma* signifies the occurrence of any action or transaction since, without it, the right or wrong deeds cannot be evaluated.

According to the definition, there are two vital aspects of ***'Karma Yoga.'*** The first one is the ***path of action*** *(which is basically a focused effort)*, and the second one is ***selfless service*** *(voluntarily foregoing own benefits for the sake of serving the human form of deity)* to be extended to others. From the definition and the elements, it can be derived that *Karma* is the multiplication of *the path of action* or focused efforts and *selfless service.*

*Karma Yoga (Action and deeds) = Path of Action X Selfless Service*

Eventually, all human resources professionals, by virtue of their assignment nature, ought to interact with internal and external customers and stakeholders. However, the nature of the connection is likely to vary widely due to environmental factors and the type of organization.

In an organization that has taller hierarchies and/or is governed by established rules and protocols, a lot of effort is required to connect with people down the line, and often, a lack of connection is reported as a factor of attrition, particularly in entry-level roles. As a rule of thumb, in traditional organizations, the paternalistic attitude of the HR is often appreciated and perceived to be a better way of connecting with employees. Listening patiently and empathizing with the concerns of an employee showcase both the ***path of action*** and ***selfless service*** as per Karma Yoga. HR can play a crucial role by creating healthy and transparent workplace practices.

Conversely, in newer organizations or organizations employing predominantly Gen Y[74] or Gen Z employees, HR professionals are more likely to focus on employee wellness and career planning through seamless implementation of talent development and talent management initiatives. As partners with the business, HR can leverage the ***path of action*** by continually evolving strategies toward higher-level retention and creating an internal talent pool through suitable hiring practices.

As an experienced HR professional, I have come up with a few suggestive tips that any HR professional can practise to satisfy the path of action and demonstrate the attitude of selfless service. I have differentiated the suggestive actions at the various phases of the Employee Life Cycle[75].

### 8.3.1. Selection Process

- The selection process is not only the process of hiring individuals for a given set of roles, but it is also the single most important process to set the tone of an organization by highlighting its brand image to the outside world. Every member of the hiring team must understand that it is not only a process of closing the numbers against vacant or new positions, but it is also the first connection between the employer and the prospective employee. Therefore, it is highly recommended that the organization should share as much information as possible with the candidates to satisfy their queries and requirements.

- There should be an initiation of the hiring process and a clear briefing about the organization and its businesses. Job Description[76] and roles should be explicitly specified without any scope of confusion.
- There should be fairness in the interview process and time. Every interview process should be well-structured, and adequate time should be offered to a candidate to settle down.
- The hiring team should be courteous enough to entertain and handle the queries just as a brand ambassador of the organization.
- Rejected candidates should be thanked for the interest shown and the time devoted by them.

It is one of the single most important phases in which the HR team accumulates good *karma* or bad *karma*. A small gesture of generosity extended to a candidate can pave the way for the whole thought process of a candidate recruited. On the contrary, small acts of arrogance towards a candidate can jeopardize a thousand good things.

### 8.3.2. Process of Recruitment

- When a candidate is on the verge of becoming an employee after passing through an interview and other selection processes, the role of the HR team increases manifold to attract, negotiate, and, quite importantly, bridge the gap between confusion and dilemma, which all of us might have faced while changing the organizations for further growth in our career. ***Karma Yoga*** plays a crucial role here as well in shaping the employee experience[77] before or after the on boarding. The suggestive plan of action can be exhaustive, but for the sake of simplification, the actions mentioned below can prove to be beneficial:

- To ensure that the recruited candidate understands the offered compensation package and can easily compare old and new packages.
- It is usual that compensation structure can differ between organizations, roles, and hierarchies, and it can be a herculean task to strike a balance between the organizations. Nevertheless, it is pertinent for the hiring team to elaborate on the offered compensation in detail without making false commitments. In the case of salary negotiations, the exercise should be a *win-win*.
- Individuals usually feel included when a few words of encouragement or gesture of care are shown to them. An HR professional can easily do so by building up a rapport by effectively using words, gestures, and body language.
- To ensure a positive employee experience, non-monetary benefits like learning opportunities and growth possibilities must be explained with the point of contact in case of any doubts.
- A periodic survey of employee experiences can provide data to understand loopholes and areas for improvement.
- After the influx of Gen Z into the workforce, it is rapidly becoming important to create value addition for a given role and establish an outcome-based objective evaluation. It is crucial to attach value to any job rather than to specify mundane operative guidelines.

- In the era of *Diversity, Equity, and Inclusion (DEI)*, HR must create an inclusive workplace by formulating, implementing, and disseminating DEI policies on or before on boarding to ensure better socialization.

It will not be an exaggeration to state that exerting a proper *path of action* and a little *selflessness* helps the entire organization create a culture of mutual trust and harmony and mitigate most employee grievances, which usually emanate from shattered dreams and loss of faith in management.

## ➢ Bhakti Yoga

*Bhakti yoga* is one of the four classical schools of *yoga* alongside *Jnana* (knowledge or self-study), *Karma* (action), and *Raja* (meditation), each offering a path to *moksha* (spiritual liberation) and self-realization.

Derived from the Sanskrit word *bhaj*, meaning "to serve God," *Bhakti yoga* is a practice of selfless devotion and recognition of the Divine in everything.

*Bhakti yoga* is one of the most common paths of spiritual development, particularly in India, where the practice originated. The concept was first described in the *Bhagavad Gita* and the *Upanishads*, ancient Hindu texts focusing on liberation from suffering.

The word *Bhakti* refers to human emotions towards God or other humans as a representation of the deity. *Bhakti* is a combination of self-awareness, self-control, and self-regulation, which can only be achieved by an individual with a higher level of maturity.

Therefore, in practice, it is the Emotional Intelligence (EI) by which an individual can not only understand, control, or regulate their own set of behaviors but can also understand the effect of their behaviors on others and appreciate others without being judgmental. One of the essential qualities for people management is emotional intelligence, and for every HR professional, it is a must to have competency across levels.

In a practical workplace scenario, HR professionals must use their high level of empathy and Emotional Intelligence (EI). Therefore, in the absence of judicious EI, there will be no inclusion or mutual trust and belief. Eventually, following ***'Bhakti Yoga'*** can lead to a high degree of Emotional Intelligence which is becoming a key tool for every HR professional of the 21st century. An HR of any organization, irrespective of the demography or industry, can reach out to any employee and touch their lives through a proper understanding of their belief and value systems affecting the work ethics on the one hand and individual aspirations, fear, or concerns on the other.

There can be a long list of HR people practising *Bhakti Yoga* at the workplace, but it may seem to sermonize them. Therefore, it is much easier for me to suggest a few actionable points that are feasible and realistic to practise.

- ***Practising Being Non-judgmental*** – It is a unique quality to assess the situation or people without attaching any pre-conceived impression. It is a higher stage of self-awareness in which, being intrinsically aware of our strengths and weaknesses, we are not required to embark upon external sources to validate our core competencies.
- ***Managing Egocentricity – Egocentricity*** is defined as thinking only about oneself without considering others' feelings and requirements. Children, particularly infants, are found to be highly egocentric as they are solely concerned about their requirements. Hence, even if they are fed timely, until and unless their next requirement is satisfied, they keep

pestering. *Bhakti Yoga* shows the path towards practising inclusion by overcoming egocentric behavior, particularly acts of high-handedness usually seen at the workplace while dealing with shop floor workers.

- ***Practise Humility at the Workplace*** – Both *Karma and Bhakti Yoga* preached the impact of mutual transaction and inclusion on any individual attached to any professional or social group. Practising both can have a strong level of emotional intelligence, which is one of the requirements of humility (*how can I help and how can I serve?*). Therefore, servility is one of the by-products of humility. It is a stage in which an individual feels inclined to serve others without considering their own benefits. Understanding others and serving their needs with an attitude of humility and corresponding servility is the crux of the *Bhakti Yoga* preachings.

Contemplation of *Bhakti Yoga* enunciates a closer look at selfless service, which is a constituent of *Karma Yoga*, and even if the path of action is positive, the overall outcome can dissipate if the objectives of the service are not beneficial for the group.

### ➢ Gyana (Jnana) Yoga

***Gyana Yoga*** talks about cognition, intellect and understanding. In the absence of this, our identity will be at stake. *Gyana Yogis* are inclined inwardly with the highest level of self-consciousness coupled with deep introspection on '*Who am I?*' and '*What am I?*'. *Gyana Yoga* teaches us mindfulness by detaching with object referral, which is defining the self through external objects, situations, titles and possessions (*Object Referral | What is? – Master Mind Matrix*).

In the Bhagavad Gita, Lord Krishna is believed to have transcended himself from the object referral. Therefore, without any doubt, he is the best coach the earthly world has ever come across. Using *Gyan Yoga* can equip an HR professional to coach or mentor people to find the answer to '*Who am I & What am I?*'. Most of the performance derailers can be coached, and they can surely overcome their problems after a certain period, provided an individual is comfortably uncomfortable with the coach assigned.

On the battlefield of Kurukshetra, the warrior prince Arjuna decided not to fight the war against the Kauravas, who were his keens and blood relations. However, he comfortably discussed the uncomfortable dilemmas with Lord Krishna, his mentor, and with his help, he overcame his hesitation and mental agony.

The workplace issues mentioned below (though not exhaustive) are the areas to develop to manage the talent and minimize the probability of quiet quitting.

- *Lack of Self-confidence*
- *Demotivation*
- *Feeling of helplessness*
- *Poor balance between work and life*
- *Lack of direction toward performance*
- *Handling interpersonal relations at the workplace*
- *Negative and destructive thought*
- *Handling crucial conversations*[78]
- *Problems in handling conflicts*
- *Fear of failures*

Not only HR but also line managers can use the techniques to manage talent and avoid costly attrition. However, before using the tools and techniques of coaching, one must be sure of one's level of self-awareness coupled with mindfulness and degree of interest in facilitating others without attaching to the object.

A closer look at the above diagram of the first page reveals that all three *Yogas (Karma, Bhakti, and Gyana)* are intertwined and work in sync.

Therefore, the maturity of any HR function depends upon:

- Transactions with individuals or groups at every stage of the employee life cycle.
- Inclusion of the individuals within the organization by penetrating the minds and hearts of people without prejudices and disruptive ego[79].
- Realizing the potential of each individual and navigating towards higher maturity to perform better.

# Chapter| 9

## Managing Human Resources and Human Relations – Integration with Organization Life Cycle

A budding human resource professional just after passing out from a *B School* may have certain dreams and aspirations that can get into concrete shape after stepping into the corporate world. However, after serving for a considerable period of time, a befuddling question can disturb the subconscious mind of any human resources professional: ***'Is it really what is aspired or dreamt of?'*** In the professional journey of human resources, it is frequently criticized that earlier, ***'HR was responsive,'*** but now, ***'HR is insensitive.'*** Sometimes, statements may take a bit different shape, such as 'when the needs of the HR are over, hardly at all they recognize us.'

Isn't it bewildering when such statements are disseminated by business leaders and even by the peer group of the same fraternity? Most of the time, HR professionals hardly pay little or no attention to it until it adversely impacts their career growth. These statements may be in absolute or relative terms or may be highly subjective, but it is worth pondering for a critical evaluation so that each such professional may have an idea and can work upon it to prove their efficacy to all the stakeholders, be it employees or the management.

In this chapter, efforts have been made to integrate how HR professionals behave in certain patterns at different stages of the ***Organization's Life Cycle (OLC)***, which is defined as a sequence of stages of growth and development through which an organization may pass (*Gareth R. Jones & Mary Mathew*). ***The Organizational Life Cycle*** is categorized into four stages, namely:

- Organizational birth
- Organizational growth
- Maturity and
- Organizational decline

In order to understand the possible behavioral outcomes of any HR professional and their interconnectedness with the ***organization's life cycle***, two variables are introduced as ***'Task Orientation[80]'*** and ***'Relationship Orientation[81]'*** to examine the pattern in different stages of the life cycle. However, this framework never claims that it is a sacrosanct one, but it will definitely help eminent readers revisit and review certain behavioral patterns. At the same time, the framework suggested below will try to elucidate and identify the connection or missing link with the organization's life cycle, which can make it somewhat easier to translate the behavioural pattern of an HR professional in a specific organizational context.

Before presenting the framework, it is pertinent to know the definition of the terms as discussed below:

- ***Task Orientation***: It connotes the tendency to focus on completing certain tasks, especially those that contribute to the success of a larger project or job. It basically focuses on meeting the deadline without considering much about how to meet it. Too much task orientation often leads to a perception of unresponsiveness towards human sentiments.
- ***Relationship Orientation:*** It is the propensity or emphasis on developing relationships with employees by positively affecting the well-being of an employee within the workplace or outside the workplace. A

person who believes in relationship orientation tries to achieve the result by maintaining a congenial work atmosphere and motivating people both formally and informally.

From the above definition, it is quite apparent that for task-oriented HR professionals, on most of the occasions, people are used as an instrument or means to achieve the desired outcomes, which can be deadline-specific; on the other hand, for Relationship HR professionals, individual relationship matters a lot and every such interaction is considered to be an experience rather than a mere transactional relationship.

However, some of the specific human resources deliverables are applicable for the specific stages of an organization's life cycle, which an HR professional has to perform, but they are labeled to be unpopular, like downsizing, staff reduction, or performance appraisal. It will be a further endeavor, using the framework mentioned below, to study the pattern of how people perceive an HR department discharging unpopular tasks cited above and how the changing life cycle of an organization affects the humane[82] face of an HR professional in due course of time.

Based on this backdrop, let us consider the framework mentioned below: '*Task—Relationship Orientation Matrix.*'

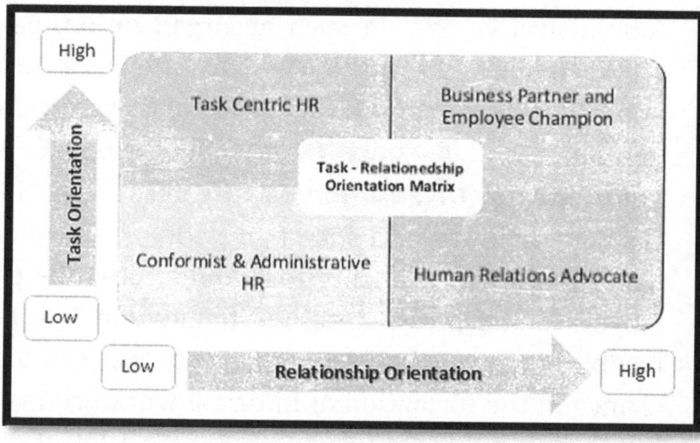


*Figure 9.1*

In this framework, based on the two variables - 'Task Orientation' plotted on the vertical axis and 'Relationship Orientation' plotted on the horizontal axis, respectively, and the degrees denoted as 'High' and 'Low', four combinations can be derived that can describe an HR professional somewhat appropriately. Each such combination is depicted below:

- ***Combination I: Low Task Orientation & Low Relationship Orientation:*** Organizations, during their birth stage, are mostly unstructured and usually operate based on individual desires or needs. In such organizations, human resources are still considered to be a cost function, and someone is deputed to HR just for the sake of obeying orders and exercising administrative decisions and controls. Such professionals can neither take the liberty to make decisions nor focus on the tasks that seem to be important from the point of view of human resources. In such a combination, HR personnel just act as the 'Yes Man' of the management. Such HR professionals are termed in the framework as 'Conformist & Administrative HR.' In such an organization, neither the ***Need*** nor the ***Speed*** of HR deliverables is important, as HR cannot decide any of these variables.

- ***Combination II: Low Task Orientation & High Relationship Orientation:*** In organizations, during their growth stage, a lot of importance is given to people centricity as people are found to be the prime movers of business. Here, we found that if a lot of flexibility is provided to employees, there is a high chance of the formation of informal work groups (e.g. Lunch group, Ladies Group, etc.) with a lot of cross-functional communication and an HR person can also take part into those informal groups. In such groups, it is evidenced that a lot of operational inputs are exchanged, issues are discussed, and thoughts are exchanged, which can be used judiciously by a successful HR to highlight the appropriate issues or maybe a tentative grievance to the management and think of the necessary redressal well before its negative ramification. Such relationship-oriented HR professionals are termed here as '*Human Relations Advocates.'* Such HR professionals can act as change agents through their employee advocacy. In such an organization, employee *Need* is given more importance than *Speed* of delivery.
- ***Combination III: High Task Orientation & High Relationship Orientation***: This combination is characterized by organization maturity, where well-laid out policies and practices, coupled with a high level of employee maturity and higher levels of IQ, make it easier for the HR professionals to focus on deadline-oriented tasks without compromising the human touch at the workplace. In such an

organization, HR professionals can be termed in this framework as ***'Business Partner & Employee Champion.'*** Such an organization philosophically takes a keen interest in harnessing employee relationships both formally and informally, so it is also an overarching requirement for respective HR to follow a similar stance. In organizations, where employee engagement is one of the keys to success, it is observed that the behavior pattern of HR personnel is shaped accordingly. In such a combination, both the *Need* and *Spee*d of HR deliverables matter most.

- ***Combination IV: High Task Orientation & Low Relationship Orientation:*** In the early declining stage, an organization, as a part of a revival strategy, tries to mitigate the decline rate of business continuity. In such cases, manpower may often be considered a cost rather than an asset. Therefore, as a trim-down measure, it becomes an overarching requirement for an organization to cut down manpower. Often, it is observed that in such organizations, completing tasks within the specified deadline becomes part and parcel of organizational life. Maybe to survive or to make oneself relevant, everyone, including HR professionals, is driven by it, and as a result, relationship orientation and human touch are lost rapidly. In such an organization, people, processes, and technology are intertwined in such a way that little scope exists for informal human interaction. In the above framework, it is labelled as '***Task-Centric HR or Mechanistic HR.'*** Only ***Speed*** of delivery is appreciated and there is no empathy for peoples' ***Needs***.

The readers can ask whether such combinations are permanent and the answer is certainly 'no' because every HR professional needs to discharge certain activities at various stages of the ***organization's life cycle***. Hence, the same HR perceived as a Good One at one stage of the life cycle may be changed as Not So Good in another stage. An organization, being an organic structure, also passes through a life cycle. Both the ***Need*** and ***Speed*** of the HR deliverables are important in some stages, whereas, in others, they may not be so important.

However, it is always the individuals who can do wonders in the practice of human resources practice. It is always preferred to use the human touch irrespective of the organization's life cycle by harnessing empathy and resilience towards both the ***Need*** and ***Speed*** of delivery to every individual concerned from induction to post-separation. Unpopular work can also be discharged with due empathy, and in today's world, where people are emotionally mature enough to understand and differentiate the humane face of an HR, the onus of making every such transaction a truly delightful one is lying to the person concerned. After all, it is our life.

# Chapter 10

## Benchmark the Career before It Is Late

Today's everyday corporate life is dynamic and always subject to disruptive changes due to changes in relationships between people and processes. These changes are restricted to process innovation and simplification of work, but they are extended to rapidly changing the business structure by pruning down the hierarchies. So, one can understand by now that incumbents for a given position are quite high, but the availability is quite low, which is creating competition among individuals to reach the coveted position. Any competition for a longer duration is more likely to attract stress burnout and health hazards since the mental setup of all the individuals is not similar, and so is their stress-bearing capacity. It is, therefore, imperative to benchmark the career, at least from the stage when it attracts stress, the feeling of obsolescence, and poor work-life or health hazards. This chapter can be used as a road map towards benchmarking the career since it is the duty of the individual to reflect upon by way of positive self-talk or by way of effective mentoring.

### *10.1. Foreword*

Each professional from campus up to the initial induction on the very first day at the workplace used to be preached by the professors of *B Schools* or the senior leaders of organizations that *The Sky is the limit* for career growth. Of course, such a utopian encouragement is applicable irrespective of the organization and its size, culture, demographic biases, etc. That set of magic words keeps buzzing around the ears of every aspiring professional participating in the corporate rat race for career growth. However, many times, it leads to only a haphazard career graph and ends up with lowered self-esteem, stress burnout, disengagement, and personal life disorders.

The question is whether the achievement of someone's career is illusive or a result of successful expectations management governed by the logical notion of one's own competence and a fair understanding of the implicit and explicit interface of individual aspirations with organizational expectations from the role or the position.

This topic will surely dive deep to find the best possible answer to this question. Since the chapter is based on individual experiences, readers may or may not agree with the thoughts and observations, but they will surely extrapolate a few of the conclusions that will help aspiring young professionals better navigate their career journeys.

*10.2. Loss of Expectations*

With the above set of contexts, let us examine the possible interfaces of individual aspirations with organizational expectations. However, these interfaces often remain unnoticed from the individual point of view, and till they surface out, it is too late to get hold of the root cause. Usually, sudden disillusion with career assignments and consequent quiet quitting pose a threat to the HR department. In most cases, the reasons for exit are ambiguous and throw little light on the root cause that might have triggered mid-level leaders to back out silently from the race, citing the reason for a career break or balancing work and life. Why do those individuals who have devoted wholeheartedly to the organizational cause by sacrificing personal lives and skipping yearly events suddenly take such a stance that leads to premature exit? The result of the exit interview will only reveal the general cause, which is majorly used as a source of data generally used for making strategic decisions on strengthening hiring and retention policies.

*10.3. Individual Aspirations*

Individual aspirations are sometimes idiosyncratic[82], especially at the beginning of one's career journey, and they usually take shape as one grows older. It is also very pertinent that tolerance towards organizational rejection (***particularly promoting someone in a leadership position or removal from a role***) is inversely correlated with seniority. Hence, the more psychological impact such a rejection will have on someone at a higher age, the greater the chances of active disengagement. The likelihood of demotivation can be higher for aged employees because they do not have enough chances of hopping from one job to another due to the predominance of safety needs. The mid-career crisis is characterized by safety needs as a pull factor coupled with a push factor governed by self-actualization. Therefore, any lack of growth in the career path detrimentally affects employees' well-being and gradually leads to disengagement.

Unfortunately, only a handful of business professionals can fix up the actualization needs out of the organizational context to stay happy with whatever is made available to them. After all, it is always preferable to grow horizontally if the vertical growth is slowing down. Therefore, setting the benchmark for someone's career is equally important because ***Everyone cannot be at the helm of the power or nearer to its source***. Therefore, it is always better to have a pragmatic approach towards one's own strengths and weaknesses that can help one grow without making unnecessary personal sacrifices or spending sleepless nights. At the same time, aspiring leaders should also be aware of the intention or the willingness of the organization to make the available opportunities grow. Eminent readers, please remember that success in the present role will not always secure the berth into the next level of leadership position until it is intended by the organization.

*10.4. Understanding the Ownership of Action*

If tolerance towards denying promotion or upliftment is inversely related to age, as mentioned in the previous section, then patience towards the rejection in career upliftment can be inversely correlated to age. Maybe that is why entry-level managers are more easily frustrated or demoralized by a single denial of promotion or upliftment. It will perhaps not be an exaggeration to say that in today's corporate world, everyone is chasing each other to reach the pinnacle of success in the least possible time. Every such growth in the career brings a change or enhancement of responsibilities and an implicit expectation attached to the higher roles. The real tragedy is that most career aspirants consider ownership or accountability of action with lesser weight. The outcome is simple and quite evident: the quality of decisions is far below the desired standard.

*10.5. The Pressure of Positional Expectations and Acceptance*

The famous works of *John C Maxwell* on the famous creation of Leadership 2.0, an interesting equation and analogy, can be used to depict the topic of the discussion. According to the author, leadership effectiveness is a multiplication of quality and acceptance.

*10.6. Effectiveness = Quality X Acceptance*

Of course, leadership effectiveness is directly related to the quality of the decisions made after understanding the present and future context that impacts the organization and suitably responding to it. Acceptance is supposed to impact the quality of the decisions. However, practically, it acts as an independent variable. Therefore, there are an ample number of instances where, despite quality decisions, a leader can be slipped off just because the decisions are not accepted by the leadership team.

To gain leadership acceptance, people mingle with the leader by dancing to the rhythm of the music or by clicking selfies with the leader. They store them in their memory bank and later utilize them in an appropriate forum to obtain group acceptance or lead a group using the power of passive influence. Focusing on the acceptance part is becoming a practice because it can compensate for the quality of decisions to maintain overall effectiveness.

It is quite disappointing that after disseminating the Western version of leadership ideology into all available leadership training or interventions, changes are very meagre in our nation, and expectations from a leader remain idiosyncratic.

Very few development managers are moving towards the upper crust of leadership, which ideally should not be the case if leadership *mantras* from the West are practised. Due to ethnocentric[83] biases, these expectations and acceptance from the top end of the leadership can vary considerably, making it tough for leaders to foresee the unforeseen.

*10.7. People Retention – HR Matters or Leadership to Take Care*

When a line employee performs, the credit is owned by the leader, but when they fail or leave, mostly HR personnel or HR activities are held liable. However, people managers are supposed to take care of the people with respect to occupational well-being and careers to feed the leadership pipeline or at least create successors.

The practical experience is different, as most of the line managers are more inclined towards chasing the targets mandated from the top, and therefore, little attention is possibly paid to people development. As a result, either the quality of successors is far below the organization's standard, or the acceptance of successors is low, and the overall effectiveness is highly questionable. It is also a well-experienced fact that whenever there are any instances of non-achievement, the following are the few criticisms that are highlighted by the line team.

- *Quality of human resources*
- *Non-availability of human resources*
- *Gap in competency*

Surprisingly, in all the above cases, the hiring team accepts the blame despite the fact that all the technical assessments are being done by the technical team.

*10.8. Career Growth – Matrix of Individual Aspirations Vs Organizational Expectations*

Based on the center stage created by this time, the focus of the balance part of the chapter will be to fix the career goal by identifying the level of individual career aspirations and possible organizational expectations from a leader.

If anyone spends a few hours pondering this aspect, there will be a shocking revelation both at an individual and organizational level that the interface is intricate, and to elaborate on the interface, a 3 x 3 matrix relationship can be a better tool to use to describe the relationship. Therefore, the two variables need further deliberation.

***Individual Aspiration***—In the corporate competitive world, where every professional is running after a coveted career, an individual's aspirations or viewpoints towards the career differ significantly over time and/or are based on realistic assumptions of both aspirations and the organization's propensity to provide the opportunity for individual progress. It will not be incorrect to summarise that individual aspiration is a function of several factors that are associated with both emotional and intelligence quotients[84].

*Individual Aspirations = f (EQ) +f (IQ)*

Therefore, it is quite understandable that based on the degree of EQ and IQ, individual aspirations can vary from low to medium to high, depending on the factors mentioned below:

*Organizational Expectation* – Any organization is a conglomeration of people; therefore, its expectations can differ from person to person who is holding the stakeholder's chair. So, a change in a dynasty brings forth changes in expectations from leaders due to numerous factors sometimes jumbled at a time. It is somewhat more complex to understand the expectations of an individual leader. It is also confusing why an organization falls in love with particular leaders and stops loving someone suddenly often without a cogent cause.

Therefore, it is tough to identify the function of organizational expectations. However, there is a likelihood that if the leadership is mature enough (having a high-level EQ), the expectations can be rational rather than laser-logical. It is equally important for a professional organization to place the leadership pipeline in place so that at any point in time, the next level of leadership is ready for the show.

Therefore, at least a rough analogical equation can be created, and it can be summarised that organizational expectation is the sum of *leadership maturity, availability of successors,* and *business environment* impacting the organization.

*Organizational Expectation = f (leadership maturity) + f (availability of successors) + f (business environment)*

Based on the above analogies, let us reflect upon the 3 X 3 X 3 matrix relationships with the variables of individual aspirations and organizational expectations. The disclaimer notes that the perspective shared is purely personal, based on two decades of professional experience in human resources.

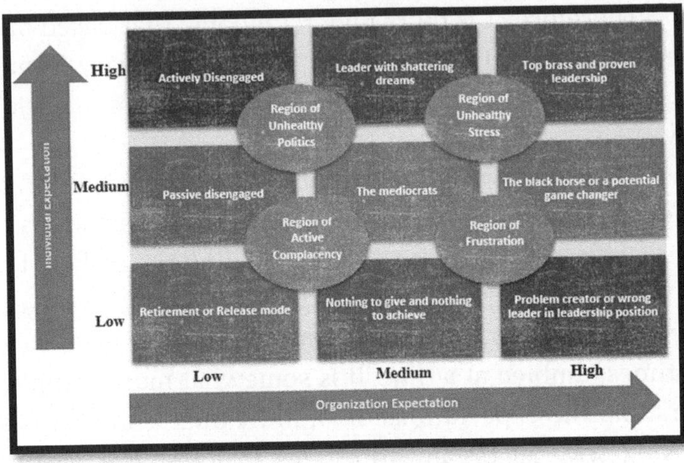


*Figure 10.1: Matrix of Individual Aspiration & Organizational Expectations*

Based on the level of ***Individual Aspiration (IA)*** and ***Organizational Expectation (OE),*** necessary combinations are plotted, from which a total of 9 combinations can be identified. In this last section of the chapter, all these possible outcomes are depicted briefly.

- ***High IA + High OE*** – The blue-eyed boys of the top leadership have all the rights and privileges over all the resources they feel necessary for achieving organizational objectives. Phenomenal career growth coupled with all recognitions is made available. However, staying at the top for a long time is always a different ballgame, and it depends heavily on several factors which are beyond the discussion of the topic.
- ***Medium IA + High OE*** – People working with medium Individual Aspiration (IA) coupled with higher Organizational Expectation (OE) are more likely to

face a crisis of work-life balance as organization expectations are high. Such people can be a dark horse with lots of potential. However, the propensity to control emotions is less, and therefore, the likelihood of Organizational Expectation (OE) can die down rapidly, and consequent growth becomes stagnant at a later stage.

- ***Low IA + High OE*** – Career growth should not be restricted only to monetary or positional growth; rather, it should be characterized by people development, process innovation, and a fair understanding of the business growth. However, the tragedy is that people are more concerned with the privilege part rather than the responsibilities and ownership of actions. Due to the higher Organizational Expectations based on past performance and/or ethnocentric biases, there are higher chances that a wrong person is identified for the potential role.
- ***High IA + Medium OE*** – In the journey of corporate life, on several occasions, we meet people with higher Individual Aspiration (IA), which is evidenced by their performance and the quality of the decisions they make. However, performers who always perform well do not ensure management acceptance, which was discussed earlier; therefore, over time, the effectiveness of such leaders receded, which can act as a further downward pull in Organizational Expectation (OE). This stage should be a crucial area for any organization to ponder upon. Otherwise, it can create disengaged managerial employees with unscrupulous work ethics[85].
- ***Medium IA + Medium OE*** – Employees who are average performers develop a mindset of mediocrity,

and the organization also does not have any high expectations from them; therefore, both sides shy away from testing the leadership capabilities. The shackle of a mediocrity mindset is very hard to break, and only very few can take the risk. Timely coaching and mentoring can prevent employees from slipping further below the quadrant.

- ***Low IA + Medium OE –*** Sustained performance of the individuals is the mantra of all the organizations. However, stagnated performance over a longer period can pull down the self-esteem of any individual to the lower side and develop a feeling of complacency, evidenced across the organizations that are used to evaluating the leader in the same performance bracket without any upgradation. The feeling of having nothing more to prove can be detrimental to the growth and sustenance of any organization.
- ***High IA + Low OE –*** A high level of Individual Aspiration (IA) always tries to push an individual toward the top. However, a poor performance track record pulls down organizational expectations. Also, there are certain departments predominantly in support functions where the scope for career growth is pegged after a certain level. As a result, people working in those areas feel a sense of insecurity and obsolescence, involving unhealthy politics.
- ***Medium IA + Low OE –*** This stage is an offshoot of the previous stage and is characterized by slow deterioration of self-esteem and passive disengagement. Employees with medium Individual Expectations (IA) and low Organizational Expectations (OE) slowly opt for detachment and leave the organization.

- ***Low IA + Low OE*** – It is noteworthy that before superannuation, irrespective of roles and seniority, people are more interested in terminal benefits for post-retirement livelihood. Therefore, career aspiration is replaced by security needs as per Maslow's hierarchy of needs theory. It is interesting to note that self-actualization[86] needs, even during the fag end of a career, in the form of career development, shift the needs to the first stage of the hierarchy of needs. At this level, nothing is expected from an employee, and the employee only expects good behavior to ensure the settlement of retirals expeditiously and a little bit of extra care from the organization. The attitude of an organization can clearly be understood by how it behaves with the people who, after spending years, leave the organization in the form of retirement.

Eminent readers can find themselves in any of the above nine combinations and reflect upon the possible short-term and long-term gains in careers made only after undertaking the necessary pain because nothing is free in this world.

Lastly, in the above 3 x 3 x 3 matrix relationship or interfaces between ***Individual Aspirations (IA)*** and ***Organizational Expectations (OE),*** four distinctive areas are identified in which there is the likelihood that any individual or group of individuals can behave in a certain fashion.

- ***Region of Unhealthy Stress*** — This region covers the upper right four quadrants in which individual career aspirations are either high or medium coupled with high to medium organizational expectations. Based on the mismatch between aspirations and expectations, individual employees try to soar by reaching closer to the power source. At the same time, people with medium aspirations find it more challenging to stay in the competition. As a result, in both cases, the likelihood of unhealthy occupational stress and unhappy personal life can be observed.

- ***Region of Frustration*** – It is a well-acclaimed fact that dramatic career growth is not everyone's cup of tea because our degree to sacrifice the family and social life differs apart from competencies and leadership skills. Therefore, if someone feels that family commitment and responsibilities are the primary focus, then reaching the pinnacle of success may be a tough ballgame, as personal factors can be a limiting factor. Most people want success with the minimum sacrifice, which can ultimately turn into frustration. In the lower four quadrants of the matrix, Individual Aspirations (IA) are medium. However, on the contrary, the organization expects more, and junior or mid-level leaders get easily frustrated as personal sacrifice does not attract the desired career success.
- ***Region of Unhealthy Politics*** – Someone may join an organization with a dream of career success, but their dream can gradually die because of the role, position, or organizational expectations (OE), which sometimes create a serious bottleneck for an individual to grow despite having the knowledge, skills and abilities. Also, there are umpteen instances of sudden decline in career growth. This can be due to the fact that most of the managers are unable to come out of managerial psychology and embrace leadership psychology. In any organizational structure, it is not at all possible to predict when a manager becomes a leader. At this level, there are high chances of indulging in unhealthy politicking because the individual perception of

distributive justice from the organization is questionable.

- ***Region of Active Complacency*** – The last left-hand quadrant is a classical depiction of when Individual Aspirations (IA) are medium to lower, and so is the case for the organization. It was discussed in detail in the previous section. The only thing that needs to be clarified is possibly some key reasons. People, particularly those who have relatively lower self-esteem and perform averagely for a long time, after a long tenure with the same organization, usually develop complacency. In some of the cases, it can be due to passive disengagement[87] or continuous denial of career growth. However, it is good for any organization if such employees are relatively fewer in number and can exit early.

In a nutshell, it can be concluded that all the above nine stages and four regions are not well-differentiated as people can change their personal, social, and organizational priorities over time. Hence, the Individual Aspiration (IA) of a Gen Z employee will differ vastly from that of an employee who is a baby boomer. The same holds for the organizational outlook to extend support for the growth of the employees.

The challenge for any organization, as per the matrix, is to keep the ***'Black Horses Engaged through'*** *(Medium Individual Aspirations & High Organizational Expectation quadrant)* proper mentoring and coaching to reinforce the aspirations and, at the same time, to support the ***'Shattered dreamers'*** *(High Individual Aspirations & Medium Organizational Expectations quadrant)* to lead a project to prove their worthiness and their ability to come out with flying colors. However, any prudent organization, whether smaller or larger, never depends on the leader's dictum, whims, or fancies to play the role. It should be process-oriented and have HR-driven exercises with a motto to develop strong leadership without creating any vacuum.

# Chapter| 11

## The Employee Moonlighting: A Paradigm Shift in Socio-economic Context

The global economy perhaps suffered the worst-ever disaster after the eruption of the COVID-19 pandemic. It badly hit both life and livelihood, leaving the mark of catastrophe across the labor market and causing harm to both employment and employability. The badly damaged sectors like airlines, hospitality, and retail chains fuelled the crisis of loss in employment opportunities due to the total collapse of the tourism industry. However, within these bleak business situations, healthcare and pharmaceutical (thanks to the COVID-19 vaccine invention) sectors recorded robust growth despite huge fatalities of healthcare professionals across the globe. Despite the recessionary trend across the sectors, business growth in e-commerce was phenomenal because the series of lockdowns compelled households to satisfy demands at the doorstep by using e-commerce platforms. Even after the pandemic, e-commerce businesses are continuously creating value for customers and satisfying them at their doorsteps. From trimming hair to fumigation at households, from arranging *Pandits* for performing *Pujas* to booking accommodation for a cozy stay at remote holiday destinations, everything is made available at the fingertips. The introduction of Work-from-home (WFH) or Remote Working, which was earlier practised widely by IT or IT-enabled services and adopted subsequently by other businesses in the form of virtual or hybrid working, has opened opportunities for individuals to explore newer sources of income to balance their financial liabilities threatened by the erosion of permanent employment, wage cut, and frizzing of increments. So, since maintaining a livelihood is important, financial insecurity created the centre stage for exploring alternatives for sustenance. Therefore, the concept of moonlighting is an offshoot of the changing organizational commitments and outlook toward an individual employee during and after the pandemic, as evidenced by the changes in people management policies of talent acquisition, management, and retention. Though promulgated for business continuity, the policy changes negatively impacted employee morale, causing the workforce, particularly the millennials and Gen Z, to shift their mind-sets toward the workplace by leveraging expertise elsewhere without hampering primary employment. The objective of the chapter is to understand the recent socio-economic shifts that possibly act as agents for the occurrence of moonlighting.

### *11.1. Introduction*

The concept of moonlighting[89] is nothing new to the corporate world; however, significant increases in its incidences, especially during the post-pandemic, nudge the HR managers to reflect upon it. In Western countries and the US, according to Deborah Sussman, the practice of moonlighting can be traced to 1977 in Canada. According to her, the rate of moonlighting grew steadily, and by 1997, women moonlighters outnumbered their male counterparts in moonlighting. According to Gartner, by the end of 2022, almost 30% of the working population engaged in moonlighting.

However, in India, the practice was disguised and widely propagated during the post-pandemic times. The practice of moonlighting was quite common among the doctors and paramedics attached to multiple clinics after the regular duty hours of the hospitals, which has benefitted society and generated additional income. In the past, there have been umpteen instances of a cross-section of employees trying to explore an alternative occupation primarily for income and gaining experiences and expertise in the field of their interest. Even for senior professionals, the practice of moonlighting has existed for decades in the form of advisory, consultancy services, or part-time faculty services to academic institutions.

A chapter published by Germany's international broadcaster reveals that more than 3 million people in Germany worked at more than one job during 2020 with the primary motive of earning extra income. Secondary employment[90] is permitted by law in Germany if the second job is outside of the main job's working hours.

The issue of employee moonlighting gained popularity only after the resumption of the business by physical presence at the workplace. The chapter has restricted the perspective of Gen Z employees because of the growing instances of reportable moonlighting.

### *11.2. Definition*

Employee moonlighting can be defined as the practice of working for another organization while committing oneself to one organization as the primary workplace, typically without the knowledge of the employer. According to the definition, three factors are worth mentioning. However, all of them are intertwined.

- *Intention to pursue an additional occupation.*
- *Intention to be devoted to the primary employer with/without hampering the performance.*

- *Intention to devote time and energy to alternative sources without knowledge of the primary organization.*

The word ***moonlighting*** may have been generated from the fact that working in the moonlight is far more comfortable than working in the daytime. Also, working during a moonlit night helps ideate more due to the freedom of the mind from the regular daytime job, which is a primary source.

### *11.3. Typology of Moonlighting*

Since the concept of moonlighting is somewhat new or can be best connoted as the *old wine in a new bottle*, identifying the types of moonlighting is somewhat elusive. Hence, so far, the overarching principle for differentiation of moonlighting is framed from a perspective of the degree of time and energy exerted by moonlighting employees on the primary source of employment.

Employee moonlighting can be ***Persistent*** or ***Transitory***. In the case of persistent moonlighting, the likelihood is very low that a second job will replace the primary one. However, for transitory moonlighting, there are greater possibilities of shifting careers.

Based on holding a parallel job in addition to the primary job roles, there are four phases of moonlighting:

- ***Blue Moonlighting***: It is fundamentally looking for a part-time job due to dissatisfaction with the current roles. However, such endeavors seldom materialize and are called blue moonlighting.
- ***Quarter Moonlighting***: When an individual devotes a little time to the second source of income to keep the primary employment intact and at the same time

reaps financial benefits from the secondary sources, the phase is denoted as quarter moonlighting.

- ***Half Moonlighting***: The third phase is characterized by devoting half of the working time to the secondary source as it provides a substantial income for a comfortable life.
- ***Full Moonlighting***: This is the last phase in which an employee is associated with the primary source of employment just to compensate for the loss of income opportunity from a second source in the future.

Finally, the practice of moonlighting can also be categorized as ***Non-Conflicted Moonlighting*** or ***Conflicted Moonlighting***. Non-conflicted moonlighting is characterized by the minimal overlap of time and professional commitment between the moonlighters and the primary employer, who adhere to ethical standards and practices. On the contrary, the conflicted moonlighting can be viewed as an erosion of commitment and ethical standards by a clear violation of psychological contract[91] and maintaining parallel sources of income. Both half and full moonlighting can take the form of conflicted moonlighting, while quarter moonlighting is an example of non-conflicted moonlighting.

### *11.4. Socio-economic Backdrop*

It is a well-accepted truth that the pandemic has perpetually changed the socio-economic fabric across the globe, and as a result, both expectations from the organization and expectations from the organizational citizens have undergone a sea change. The eminent readers from academia and the corporates perhaps noticed the disruption across the sectors, which permanently changed both the people and the processes. Perhaps the most disruptive changes are observed among Gen Z and millennials toward work ethics by questioning the purpose of work.

A survey conducted by **Gartner** about the changes in the employee mindset that the pandemic imprinted permanently reveals some glaring results summarized below:

- *65% of the respondents strongly felt a changing attitude towards value aspects of the outside.*
- *65% of the respondents strongly agreed that the place where they work should have some influence on someone's life.*
- *62% of the target population strongly felt toward bigger change in life.*
- *58% of the respondents expressed a change in their perspective on the desirability of workplace location.*
- *56% of the sample size strongly opined for contributing to society.*
- *52% strongly questioned the purpose of the day-to-day job.*
- *50% of the population strongly agreed that expectations towards the employer have changed.*

Another survey conducted by the Randstad on Employers' Brand research survey conducted during the year 2019, which was before the pandemic, shows that the top three criteria for choosing an employer are:

- *Approximately 47% of the respondents shared that it is the salary and benefits.*
- *Approximately 46% of the population felt that work-life balance can be the second-best criterion.*
- *Approximately 41% of the people felt that job security is important.*

The survey reveals further the top three reasons for quitting a job. It is very surprising to note that the factor contributing to Gen Z employees leaving their jobs is seemingly different from the factor for which they used to join an organization. According to the study, the following factors governed the quitting of a job:

- *Approximately 43% of Gen Z felt that a restricted career path is responsible for leaving a job.*
- *Approximately 36% cited that poor work-life balance contributes to leaving the job.*
- *Approximately 33% of the target population felt that salary and fringe benefits are responsible for voluntary attrition.*

The above two surveys of **Gartner** and **Randstad** indicated a few aspects of the occupational life of Gen Z.

- Purpose of pursuing a job, whether for rewards or philanthropy.
- Balancing both work and family life is one of the guiding factors to sticking to a job.
- Career progression has remained to be a factor in the retention of Gen Z or millennials.

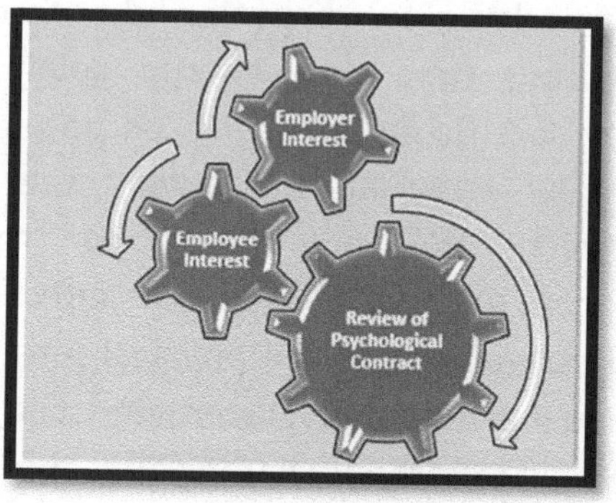


*Figure 11.1*

*11.5. Issue of Trust – Revisiting the Psychological Contract (The Gear Wheel Diagram)*

Psychological Contract refers to the unwritten set of expectations of the employment relationship, distinct from the formal, codified employment contract. Taken together, the psychological contract and the employment contract define the employer-employee relationship. It would not be an exaggeration to say that the whole HR ecosystem is substantially governed by this psychological contract, which acts as an invisible knot between the employer and the employees. Therefore, any slightest changes can destabilize the relationship and make or largely break the business's success.

Employee moonlighting is also considered an issue that is challenged by most employers on the grounds of violating the psychological contract between the employer and the employees. The possible reason for this is the mutually conflicting interests, particularly visible during the pandemic. On the one hand, downsizing is made in the name of restructuring or repositioning, and on the other hand, to sustain business continuity, the same or higher targets with lesser team size make the working environment intolerable. This leads to revisiting the psychological contract between the stakeholders, resulting in disputing the traditional work ethics of devoting time and energy solely to a single organization by sacrificing underutilized potentialities. From the standpoint of trust and reviewing the psychological contract between the employer and the employee, moonlighting can be considered an effect of changing organizational strategy from the physical interface to digital or actual to virtual connectivity, leveraging a huge potential to learn and to earn without hampering the primary role demand.

### *11.6. Experimenting and Experiencing – The Hallmark of Gen Z That Facilitates Moonlighting*

Being the ***digital natives***[92]**,** Gen Zs are inherently hyper-receptive towards trying a new way of doing things in the personal and professional sphere. The choice of experiencing by exploring a newer method of doing any task has challenged the traditional mindset. Most of the Gen Z, by virtue of their tech savviness are conscious of the outside world with respect to challenges to face and opportunities to explore, thanks to the booming flow of information technologies. As a result, the generation is characterized by impatience or uncompromising with respect to their rights and privileges, as evidenced by their aversion to working for an organization with strenuous duty hours and little scope for learning or peer group fun. Due to this trait, Gen Zs are more likely to contribute to an organization that values innovation and flexibility, irrespective of the size and brand value of the organization. Possibly, this can be a cause of why lots of Millennials and Gen Zs left their regular job and started associating with start-ups since the opportunities for innovation and learnability are much higher than the established businesses.

There is a drastic shift in traditional work hygiene factors like ethics, commitment, and loyalty towards work and personal life. It would not be an exaggeration to say that Gen Zs or millennials are progressively inclined towards experimenting and experiencing life now to energize their growth mindset[93]. The positive side is challenging the *status quo* and stretching the limit, leading to the germination of innovative ideas that benefit the organization. However, on the flip side, there was impatience in finding the purpose of any job, a quick distraction from mundane affairs, and loss of job interest due to restricted learning opportunities.

Gen Zs are more prone to raising questions about traditional operating procedures, protocols, or work ethics; hence, traditional brand value or monetary benefit is not the sole determinant for their retention. Therefore, the likelihood of moonlighting is much higher among Gen Z employees as their motto is not only to earn more money but also to explore growth paths by continuously experimenting and experiencing the areas of interest to discover the purpose of pursuing a career. Perhaps the continuous experimentation and experience lead to a higher risk appetite for the Millennial and Gen Z population, which is evidenced by the growth in the number of start-ups during this phase.

From this standpoint, pursuing employee moonlighting can energize the purpose by utilizing potential and learning skill sets that can be used to harness present and future growth prospects. It is undoubtedly true that the *Industrial Revolution 4.0* is having a causal impact on the growth of moonlighting activities.

### *11.7. Exploring the Alternative Source of Income – Safeguarding the Economic Uncertainty*

During the pandemic, we all experienced that the more insecurity there was, the greater the propensity to secure that insecurity. It was possibly the worst financial crisis in the recent past that we have experienced during the pandemic. One of the biggest lessons learned by human beings during the pandemic is to identify their potential and monetize it based on the available opportunities. Therefore, during the pandemic, people explored extra income for basic sustenance like repaying EMI, credit card bills, and children's tuition, and post-pandemic, it has become a choice for earning extra sum to fulfil their dreams. Particularly in the group of millennials and Gen Zs, who are brought up in financial affluence by fully enjoying life with expensive gadgets or spending holidays abroad, the word 'sacrificing' or 'compromise' sounds weird and hence cannot be continued for a long time.

According to the statistics published by the Indian census for the year 2011, 45.4 crores of the population settled outside their original native place, compared to 31.5 crores during the census period 2001. According to the study conducted by Ernst & Young, 67% of Baby Boomers[94] have professionally active partners, whereas the percentage of professionally active partners for Gen X and Gen Y is hopping to 86% and 90%, respectively. Furthermore, the study has revealed that 56% of couples have responded that the income of the partner is significant for lifestyle maintenance. This shift in the socio-economic pattern has brought a major change in the consumption pattern of the household.

Throughout the pandemic, due to the loss of employment, there was a subsequent reduction in household income, particularly in twin-income couples. However, the cost of living and expenses almost remained the same with respect to payment of EMI for a house, personal or car loans, or instalment of SIPs [95], which demands an exploration of the additional flow of funds to cater to livelihood expenses. Due to these changing demands, there has been a steep increase in moonlighting of women employees, making it a secret door to maintaining financial freedom.

### *11.8. Self-Actualization – Unearthing the Underappreciated Potential*

The last few years were horrible in respect of protecting the lives of the near ones and maintaining their livelihood by balancing work and life. However, in that gloomy and challenging situation, a crucial breakthrough understood the self in a much better way than ever before. A feeling of isolation from the workplace despite prolonged hours of Work from Home coupled with detachment from all social activities and a dreadful picture of the outside world instrumentalized the early attainment of self-actualization. Gen Zs and Millennials, due to their higher degree of motivation, quickly developed the path for self-development, which has furthered higher income potentiality.

Due to the traditional sociological factor in our country, choices of higher studies are still controlled by the parental dictum, which at the later stage of a career can prove disastrous or cause discontent. There are plenty of examples of students getting frustrated after joining directly from the campus. The reason for dissatisfaction can be manifold; however, the principal reason is a lack of identification with the job due to the limited scope of learning and/or job profile not commensurate at all with the specialization opted for during higher education. Partially, these employees are geared back toward higher studies to try their luck, and a balance may opt for moonlighting to gather adequate experience in their chosen field before detaching themselves from the primary organization.

Therefore, the employer must understand the root cause of moonlighting rather than imposing punitive measures or changing the appointment clauses. In the world of information availability and social networking, there is always a leeway for converting interest or acquired skills into earning potential.

### *11.9. Freedom from Boredom by Creating Value for Society*

The strenuous part of WFH or remote working is the feeling of boredom and isolation due to prolonged work schedule. One good way to get rid of work monotony is to respond to societal requirements. The horrific experiences of the COVID catastrophe perhaps made us revisit the purpose of life and serving back to society. In the Gen Z population, there is a growing consciousness towards serving society due to a higher degree of cause motivation[96]. Therefore, such populations can indulge themselves in social responsibility activities to respond to collective needs, and in the process, also overcome stress. Several such social initiatives consequently fructified into start-ups and created value for society by employing unskilled and semi-skilled manpower, particularly in the village and semi-urban areas.

However, tools to identify the exact cause of moonlighting are still in their primitive stages. Therefore, the analysis of the possible cause is biased and solely indicative of monetary gains.

*11.10. Concluding Comments*

Ideally, the issue of moonlighting should not be treated as a problem. Rather, it is causal to the socio-economic shift in the paradigm challenging the traditional employer and employee relationship, which has been permanently disrupted due to changes in the entire business ecosystem.

The traditional people-driven organizations are replaced by the process-driven ones, which has, to a large extent, brought a shift in the mindset of working populations and the organization. It is the maturity of the organization to take cognizance of moonlighting and respond with utmost care rather than weakening the psychological contract by adding non-compete[97] clauses of employment. For this reason, several organizations have allowed moonlighting as a strategy to retain talents, which has brought good results as well. In the era of the digital explosion, where everyone has access to data, knowledge, and networking, total renunciation of moonlighting can never be possible except for a few industries like construction, metal, and heavy engineering, which mandatorily demand the on-site physical presence of employees with specified duty hours as per statute.

However, the ball is in the court of the organization to design, develop and implement the people management policies equipped with the mechanism to check and control employee moonlighting not only from the standpoint of ethical practice but also to help employees control their wellness, which is negatively impacted due to prolonged hours of moonlighting by sacrificing family commitments. It is, therefore, a challenging task for the HR leaders of 2023 to concentrate more on reimagining the workplace by ensuring better employee experiences and employee connection by managing career trajectories for aspiring talents to accelerate growth for a better tomorrow.

# Chapter| 12

## People – Organization – Job: Fitment Challenges and Possibilities

The journey through the corporate world is fascinating and often complicated as well. By the time someone is approaching the coveted destination, there can be a high probability of individual heartbreak for missing the final bus towards the dream destination, which may culminate in stress burnout and a sense of redundancy or isolation. The eminent readers can easily visualize a few situations when leadership expresses concern for employees who used to perform well above the threshold level in the past but have been failing repeatedly after getting promoted to a higher level. The questions are: What goes wrong with these performers? Why is their performance suddenly slipping down? Are there any changes in the outlook of the organization towards the employees or their performance?

Unfortunately, such suitability disconnects result from a mismatch in expectations between the position/role one holds and job/role demands. On most occasions, an individual with even moderate emotional intelligence will never sense when such a mismatch will transpire, and by the time it is perceived by the individual, the organization stops showering its care and affection on the individual in question! Doesn't this comment sound a bit sarcastic?

It is a well-appreciated fact that any organization is basically a mere replication of a family. All the characteristics of a family with shared beliefs, values, norms, and collective perceptions are also present in any organization, irrespective of the size, business, demography, or the nature of the management style. Due to this characteristic, some organizations (obviously the members of the organization entrusted to make decisions) are vulnerable to falling in love with individuals or groups of individuals who are beneficial in the short run but can prove to be counterproductive for the organizational interest in the long run. Most of the time, such costly mistakes endanger organizational interests and create an unhealthy work culture. There are ample examples where initial hiring was done for ***P-J fit (Person-Job)***, but very few of the population reached the level of ***P-O fit (Person-Organization***). ***P-J fit*** refers to the match between an employee's knowledge, skills, abilities, and requirements of the job.

***Formidable challenge is neither about infusing fresh blood into the organization to make it more sustainable in long run nor it is bad to cross pollinate the organization by using diverse talent pool; but the quality of blood that is supposed to flow through organizational systems must be checked and validated before putting it into actual use as it can make or break the whole organization***

On the other hand, ***P-O** fit* refers to the match between an employee's personal values and the values of the organization. Since P-J fit alone cannot predict or validate the ethical standard of behavior of an employee, on several occasions, individuals with a higher degree of self-aggrandizement can easily manipulate the stakeholders to accept the decisions in their favor but in the long run, the mere presence of such individuals can even ruin the organizational interest, and by the time organizations locate or pinpoint the pain area, such individuals or group of individuals leave the organization after quenching their thirst.

Organizations in the digital era are used to being inclined towards innovative ideas, changing culture, and lesser human intervention. Therefore, they can be easily attracted to those who are propagating the same and make the mistake of hiring people without proper validation and reference checks. The formidable challenge is neither about infusing fresh blood into the organization to make it more sustainable in the long run nor is it bad to cross-pollinate[98] the organization by using a diverse talent pool. However, the quality of blood in the organizational blood stem must be checked and validated before putting it into actual use, as it can make or break the whole organization. The biggest irony is that while diffusing the bad blood, occasionally, good talents are sacrificed silently, making the organization less viable in the long run.

The contention of the topic of discussion is to understand the dynamics that can create potential challenges for the organization to handle good talents with care and at the same time, based on the set context, some ponderation can be done on various factors that are creating a major detachment between the employer and the employee, which in turn, adversely affects group dynamics process and can even stop the growth of the organization by making it decline rapidly.

*12.1. Perspective of Organization – Job Fit*

It is worth pondering to reflect upon *Person–Job Fit and Person–Organization Fit* and their impact on work behaviors and culture fitment, through which employees can be attached in meaningful ways and add value to one another.

It is essential for any employee to be indoctrinated with job and performance standards vis-à-vis organizational shared values, work ethics, and established performance norms; therefore, P-O and P-J fitment are equally important indicators for the sustained performance of the employees.

The presence of both factors can create ***organization-job (O-J) fit*** employees who can perform on a sustained basis and meaningfully contribute towards the achievement of overall organizational goals and objectives. It has to be kept in mind that both factors, though independent, are significantly interconnected with each other.

The ***Figure 1 Venn diagram*** represents the interconnectedness of P-O and P-J fit. It is important to understand that none of the parameters can solely predict the discretionary effort exerted by an employee in the form of performance or engagement at work. Therefore, only a cross-section of the organizational population that fits in both these aspects can be labelled as ***Organization-Job Fit (O-J Fit)***.

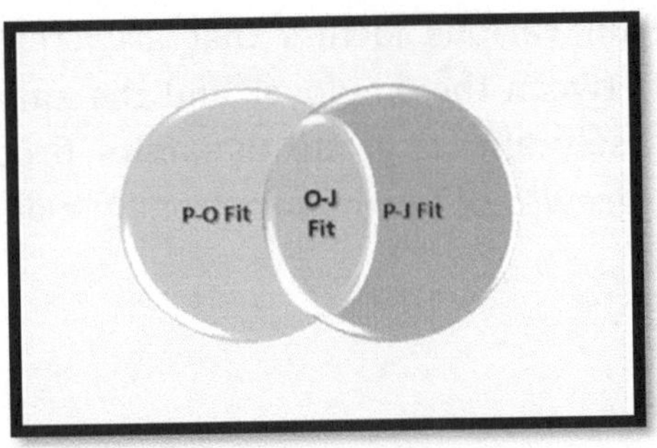


*Figure 12.1*

*12.2. Organization – Job Fitment: Expectation Paradox*

According to the above concept, the group of employees who are ***organization-job fit*** are not supposed to leave the organization. However, in reality, it is otherwise. The biggest threat of attrition is posed by the people who are O-J fit but opt to leave the organization, particularly in the middle management level, and most of the time, on the verge of idiosyncratic expectations from the position and/or choice of assignment which is faulty or deliverables which are either highly intangible or already messed up with little chance of improvement. Erosion of O-J fit employees can cause a massive erosion of organizational sustainability, creating a manpower mix of ***Person–Organization fit (P-O fit)*** and ***Person–Job fit (P-J fit)*** with a culture mediocrity. Since two distinct groups often operate in isolation by creating dysfunctional competitions, it is not for them to ensure meritocracy. O-J fit people can act as a bonding agent between the two sects of employees, and the absence of these people creates a lack of linking factor.

*12.3.* ***HARD Framework: Cyclical Process of Talent Inclusion to Redundancy***

Though the creation of the framework is entirely based on the two decades of the experiential journey of the author, careful contemplation can reveal certain aspects which can justify or substantiate initial hiring ***(when P- J fitment is high, but P-O fitment is low)*** to sense of dejection of an employee when both the factors are found to be at the lower end. The process is cyclic in nature with four possible stages, and in every employee life cycle, all or at least a few of the stages can be evidenced.

12.3.1. Stage I

The stage is characterized by the mutual happiness of both the employer and the new employee. At this stage, a candidate is hired after their credentials are checked and competencies are examined through a structured hiring process. Therefore, hiring can only be completed once the incumbent is found to be ***Person- A fit***. Since the person who is joining can be from another organization or fresh from the campuses, the predictability of ***Person–organization fitment*** cannot be validated, and hence, it is low. During the initial months of induction, which can also be termed the 'honeymoon period,' the organizations usually restrict their expectations from the job holders. However, at this stage, fresh blood comes into the organizational flow; therefore, it is very important for the organization to segregate the quality of blood in the flow, particularly in the case of bulk hiring. The following points can be considered to ensure good quality hiring:

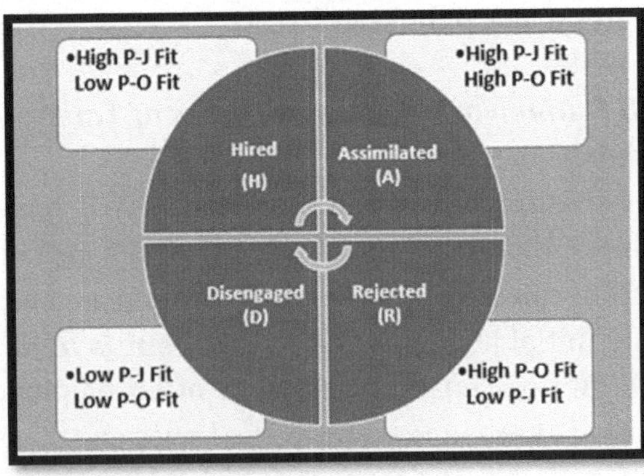


*Figure 12.2*

- ***Structured Job Description*** – It is important to understand the required skill sets, both technical and behavioral, for the job/role. A well-formulated job description with proper job element analysis can also determine the proficiency level of the role against which the candidate can be checked. This is a mandatory requirement for talent acquisition professionals to balance the quality with the quantity of hires. Also, it is always preferred to conduct interviews based on BEI[99] (Behavioural Event Interview) to understand the proficiency levels of technical and behavioral skill sets.

- ***Managing Expectations*** – It is always preferred to set the right tone for new entrants by showing a realistic picture of the role and the organization. On numerous occasions, talent acquisition teams, due to the urgency of closing positions, use the practice of over-commitment, particularly concerning compensation and fringe benefits, as well as the work culture of the organization. It is also equally important to understand the expectations of the fresh recruits to strike a balance between the employer and the employees from the initial stage.
- ***Psychometric Assessment*** – Though costly, the organizations can have the choice of using psychometric[100] tools to assess the quality of leadership hiring or hiring for niche skills in which attrition can be costly for the organization. Tests like ***MBTI[101] / FIRO-B[102]*** can play crucial roles in understanding the personal dimension of an employee and the level of extroversion/ introversion and other relevant behavioral tendencies and patterns to benchmark with the job/role expectations based on structured competency mapping.
- ***Background Verification by External Agencies*** – An impartial reference check can always be a source of various work habits and integrity of any incumbent who is hired laterally. In case of negative feedback from the

last employer, further probing is necessary to understand the authenticity. It is always suggested that Back Ground Verification[103] exercise be completed parallel to the selection process to elicit necessary information before formal offer letter generation.

- ***Faster Organizational Inclusion*** – Due to the high fitment with the role/job but low organizational assimilation process, the risk of employee turnover can be the highest, and hence, it is pertinent for any organization to adopt a well-organized induction plan for faster orientation and on boarding.

### 12.3.2. Stage II

It is the stage of assimilation and orientation of an employee to immerse into the organizational current. The more familiarized the employees are with the culture and climate of the organization, the faster the ***person-organization fit*** will be. Stage II is characterized by harmonious job and organization fitment. Most of the operational level managers or supervisors fall into this category. Since the deliverables are mostly mundane and organizational expectations are not sky-high, there is not much competition, and it is relatively easy to achieve career success. In stage II, career progression germinates through the identification of talents. A note of caution must be adopted here to identify the talents because there are several instances in which the non-deserving candidates were moved into the leadership pipeline, which caused much damage to the organizational operation and hindered the achievement of organizational business objectives. Adoption of a few initiatives can prevent the organization from committing costly mistakes.

- ***Identification of Talent*** – Who can be treated as a talent? This seems to be an innocuous question, but it is an uphill task for any organization to define talent based on the business context and identify them for further polishing towards leadership. Organizations spend a lot on leadership development initiatives, structured mentoring, and holding assessment centers. However, due to faulty definition and identification processes, such talents are unable to pass through the development centre competencies required for leadership roles. It is crucial for an organization to define and nurture talents at the supervisory level rather than at the leadership level to prevent their dropping out of the development centre.
- ***Goal-Setting Process*** – Performance parameters must be objective and quantifiable, and they should follow the ***SMART (Specific-Measurable-Achievable-Realistic-Time-Bound) guidelines*** for goal-setting exercises. Also, Key Performance Indicators (KPIs) must be well-defined to capture performance without any data fabrication. A proper performance review process can help the organization develop and retain a talent pool.
- ***Succession Planning*** – Any organization cannot sustain itself in a vacuum and needs both a leader and a group of deserving followers to maintain equilibrium. Professional organizations must work on succession planning[104] to nurture and develop future leaders at any given point of time. One of the objectives of succession planning is to create a pool of human resources who are ***Organization–Job fit*** as these are acting as a building block between P-O and P-J fits.

### 12.3.3. Stage III

Why is a consistent performer unable to perform after a promotion or maybe after a change in the role? What turns a performer from an asset to a liability for an organization? This stage can try to find out some justifications for the above queries. It is worth mentioning in this context that every elevation in the organizational hierarchy brings about a shift in expectations, and role demand gets redefined. These changes in expectations are mostly behavioral in nature, e.g. leadership capability, achievement orientation, change management, decision-making ability, and so on. When someone moves towards a leadership role, requirements for technical competence gradually take the back seat as it is presumed to be a ***'MUST.'*** However, employees from ranks usually find it tougher to come out from silos with distinct behavioral competencies, which causes the failure of expectations. Gradually, such a population starts feeling suffocated due to the role expectations despite higher ***Person – Organization fitment***. Another contributing factor is ***complacency syndrome***, which is a tendency to take the job and the organization for granted. That can be reflected in the job behavior by undermining the desired set of competencies required for the role to perform. Since it is a big challenge for any organization to keep such employees relevant for a longer period, a few suggested actions can be thought of.

- ***Transparent Feedback Process*** – A timely and objective feedback process can always set the right context and expectations between superiors and subordinates. However, it is a debated topic in some of the organizations where jobs are being carried out by the self-managed team or where pinpointing the exact contribution from the individual is somewhat dicey; there can be a high probability that the feedback process can be subjective or a mere formality.

Nevertheless, a strong feedback mechanism helps people understand the gap in performance and how far an employee grows with the organization.

- ***Job Rotation*** – Planned job rotation[105] based on the competencies can be another option by which attempts can be made to utilize such manpower and churn the talents.

### 12.3.4. Stage IV

Lack of recognition and rejection from the organization can play a big role in the deterioration of morale and motivation. Such deadwoods mostly comprise disengaged employees who gradually become misfits for the organization and the roles. It is important to understand and appreciate that not all the deadwoods are bad for the organization, as many of them are victims of dysfunctional politics despite their good performance. A question can be raised: Can this population again be a part of the organizational mainstream? Ideally, the answer is 'Yes.' They can be a part of the organizational mainstream, but hardly any organizations attempt to implement them because of the obscure effectiveness of such initiatives. However, the suggested action can be:

- ***Talent Inclusion Program*** – Talents can prevail at any stage of one's career in active or hibernated form, and their sustenance depends on the mutual intention of both the employer and the employee. From the organization's standpoint, an external counselling mechanism can be one activity by which it can clarify the intention to recycle the few deserving deadwoods into the mainstream.

Organizations are a conglomeration of people and processes where people are the prime movers and can be capable of performing wonders by churning talents in every phase of the organization's life cycle. Therefore, an organization can only be business-relevant if it can identify, develop and nurture talents through a culture of inclusivity. It is expected that eminent readers can relate to and contemplate various aspects that have been offered in the topic of discussion and find some of the aspects that can be strategized to streamline the talent pool so that it can deliver the output by judicious use of resources. It is never too late for an organization and its employees to seek and extend support to each other for mutually beneficial outcomes.

# Chapter| 13

## Managing Expectations of the Silent Performers

*13.1. The Context and Connection*

Predominantly, Indian industries were manpower intensive, and despite the mechanization of operations, there were umpteen scopes for manual operation on and off the shop floor or in a traditional engineering project. The involvement of information technology in operations brought a considerable change in labor distribution by reducing and, in some cases, replacing manual human intervention, which paved the way for the third Industrial Revolution. According to the McKinsey report, before 2014, people were hardly aware of the term Industrial Revolution 4.0; however, by 2019, as per the same report, 68 percent of the respondents globally shared a view that it is a top strategic priority, and 70 percent of the working population agreed that the organization they are working for are either piloting or implementing the digital changes in the business actions.

However, the triggering factor for businesses to promote digitalization in everyday operations was the COVID-19 pandemic.

Potential challenges for business continuity were lurking under the unlocking of the business process and market demand. It was becoming pertinent for businesses to embrace the Industrial Revolution 4.0 to remain relevant and continue. Handling tapering down business growth coupled with higher overhead costs, specifically manpower costs, mandated businesses to revisit their existing business models.

Adopting digital transformation was necessary for better predictability of business outcomes by controlling, sustaining, and improving the input, processes and, finally, quality of output. In the world of continual improvement for greater business success, gradual dependence on manpower is being replaced by digital adoptions, such as predictive analytics/ Augmented Reality[106]/ Internet of Things (IOTs)[107] and robotics, at various stages of manufacturing and service and even in complex construction activities. Using data through power BEI dashboards facilitates prompt business decisions by pinpointing the potential areas of challenge and conceivable mitigation plans. Consequent to digital adoption, capturing data on employee productivity is getting easier, resulting in more transparency in evaluating performance against the quantifiably set standard.

To be in sync with the techno-commercial demands of the industry, the recruitment strategy has also undergone major changes. Attracting, recruiting and managing talent for a longer period of time seems to be a challenging task for any HR team. Unarguably, from a business perspective, encouraging meritocracy across industries occupied the front seat. Ring-fencing the right talent is now a hot topic of discussion at every symposium or conference, and at the workplace, unique retention strategies are created for the chosen few across the globe.

Possibly, the biggest irony for any organization is that the mediocre employees want to stay with the organization for a longer period of time, whereas chosen superheroes usually leave after serving for a short stint. Still, developmental strategies are predominantly for the talented few, while the mediocre employees are struggling with a wide skill gap.

### *13.2. Silent Performers*

Before digging deep and finding out the answers to the above questions, it is obvious for the eminent readers to know what is connoted through the phrase **'Silent Performers.'** They are the employees who are critical for any organized operations manual or otherwise with moderate performance, but usually, their efforts and outcomes remain unnoticed in administering reward, recognition, and developmental opportunities. There are higher probabilities that **'Silent Performers'** demonstrate either some or all the below attributes:

- They feel a psychological attachment to the organization.
- They and their families feel social pride.
- They have a lower degree of expressiveness and/or presentation skills.
- They contribute and support the leadership team to achieve targets.
- They maintain satisfactory performance, irrespective of rewards and recognitions, to a certain extent.
- They extend support from the backend without making their presence felt.
- They handle criticality without any amplification of their accomplishments to the management.

The mind-boggling question is: Are all mediocre performers performing averagely since the beginning of their employment tenure, or is there any causal relationship between the performance vis-à-vis expectations from the organization? Though it is not very easy to prove the relationship due to the interplay of various subjective and objective factors, an attempt can be made empirically to identify the interconnectedness.

### *13.3. Expectation-Performance Linkage*

It is observed that when any employee starts performing well, the expectation of management grows exponentially and the employee is initially recognized. Reward and recognition always act as enablers for a higher level of performance. As a result, the performance level of the employees can reach the individual threshold limit, beyond which the performance level can decrease due to several factors, which are as follows:

- ***Individual*** – Every individual has a threshold limit of performance, and surpassing or even sustaining the threshold for a longer period can be challenging even for an excellent employee because continuously challenging the limit impacts health and stress burnouts.
- ***Organizational*** – HR strategy for talent identification and management can directly affect workforce morale and performance levels. One factor is talent exclusivity[108], which will be discussed in the next section.
- ***Environmental*** – Business environments relentlessly shape or reshape short- and long-term organizational priorities. Furthermore, they impact the existing HR philosophies regarding talent profiling and development strategies. They also emphasize digitalization, which affects the organization and triggers the abolition of manual workers, e.g., stenographers and surveyors.
- ***Contextual*** – Performance is always based on the context or a set premise, and any disruptive changes directly contribute to the enhancement or fall in the performance outcome.

Based on these four elements, an illustration can be drawn through a simple graphical representation (Figure 13.1). The graph is demarcated into three stages:

- **Stage 1:** This stage is characterized by exponential growth in the performance level of the employees and consequent growth in the expectation of the management. So, every Δ (delta) change[109] in actual performance (**denoted as A-P**) level is coupled with an increase in performance expectation (**denoted as P-E**) of the management. Hence, it can be concluded that at this stage, silent performers perform at a higher level as **Δ change in A-P value > Δ change in P-E value.**

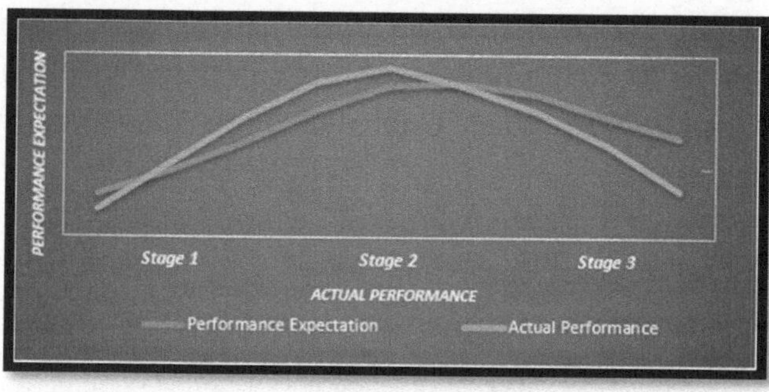


*Figure 13.1: Expectation – Performance Linkage*

- **Stage 2**: At this stage, the performance of the job holder is found to be on the higher side of their Actual Performance (A-P), but there are negative trends in the performance growth. However, Performance Expectation (P-E) is found to be on the higher side, and there is a break-even that can be called **Expectation – Performance** break-even. Here, the first jolt is observed by the job holder and the management with respect to performance. From the employee side, it is the maximum threshold limit where someone can operate based on given skills and competency factors, and from the perspective of the organization, the theory of meritocracy is actually landing into mediocrity.

- **Stage 3**: This stage is portrayed as a significant fall in Actual Performance (A-P value) coupled with a fall in Performance Expectation (P-E value). However, the rate of fall in Performance Expectation (P-E value) is much lower than the rate of fall in Actual Performance (A-P value).

So, at this stage, it is observed that **Δ change in A-P value < Δ change in P-E value.** In figure 13.1, a visual difference is shown, which signifies loss of expectation by the management towards the performance outcome of the job holder and consequent drop in the performance level of the job holder. As a culmination of this gap between Performance Expectation and Actual Performance, the following outcomes are observed:

- Organizational culture of ***Talent Exclusivity***
- Adverse outcome on performance reward
- Lack of career growth or tapering down career path
- Lack of developmental opportunities
- Less important roles and responsibilities

Lots of passive grievance and resentment come up at this stage and are vented by an employee through:

- Disengagement
- Perception of unfair distributive justice[110]
- Negative attitude towards new initiative
- Feeling of managerial obsolescence[111]
- Exit from employment.

One of the biggest problems across industries is not only retaining high performers or leaders but also developing and retaining good 'Followers' who relentlessly support the leaders in writing their success stories. So, it is also critical for HR managers to identify, develop, reward, and retain this population, failing which organizations may lose the backbones or potential backend supports.

Here, the question that is tough to answer is how to earmark a 'Silent Performer.' Is it solely a performance rating system that can differentiate a silent performer, or is there something else? Most often, silent performers are overlooked due to the reasons listed below:

- *Lack of Self-advocacy* – Employees with lower to moderate assertiveness usually shy away from voicing out or can propagate for self-achievement using available communication channels and prefer to remain silent followers.
- *Lack of Role Clarity* – Handling poorly differentiated or overlapping assignments like front office operation coupled with office stationery handling hampers taking individual responsibility for the outcome produced.
- *Lack of Self-esteem* – It is a subjective perception of an individual about their own worth and ability. However, protracted manual operations with extended duty hours coupled with poor supervisory control can lower individual self-esteem.
- *Limitation in De-skilling and Re-skilling* – The scope of training is often restricted for employees possessing niche skills. Maybe that is why a production engineer gets a higher scope for developmental intervention (both technical and behavioral) than a hardware engineer, who handles the control room hardware operation but remains a laggard despite the efforts.
- *Less Tangibility of Outcomes* – Pinpointing the excellent and mediocre performers within a Self-

Managed Team (SMT)[112] frequently becomes a challenging task for managers and HR. Organizations embarking on the forced distribution method of performance appraisal can hardly capture the exact contribution of an employee, resulting in a lack of interest in performing above the threshold.

Unfortunately, the worthiness of silent workers is felt at the last stage, when retention becomes difficult. It is a fact that when a disgruntled employee decides to quit, it is virtually impossible to ensure retention.

*13.4. Conclusion & Suggested Plan of Action*

The distinguished readers may ask whether an organization should have an exclusive talent development program to create a talent-inclusive culture by owning developmental responsibility. Maybe the answer would be 'YES' because talent is present in every individual working with any organization, and they should get an equal opportunity to develop and hone their competencies based on the job requirements (as per Talent Inclusivity School of Thought). The talent-inclusive culture promotes organizational commitment towards its employees by nurturing the potential of everyone and satisfying the '*highest needs of the individual.*'

Before organizations devise the tools for retention, the culture and outlook of the organizations should be shifted from talent exclusivity to talent inclusiveness. However, a more realistic way of managing those hidden talent banks is to reinforce the lower self-esteem through structured intervention. The traditional individual development model of 70:20:10 (70% Experiential Learning[113], 20% Social Learning[114], 10% Classroom learning) may not serve the purpose since these performers underwent sufficient experiential learning, and adding some more will be viewed as an additional burden. Ideally, counselling and effective mentoring can create an atmosphere of self-discovery through self-reflection.

Therefore, it is suggested that talents should undergo a series of social and classroom learning to feel inclusivity. Even though, in this way, only a small proportion of employees can be covered through a talent management program, at the same time, the organization can scan out top brass of talents from a bigger population. The talents found may be suitable for the organizational business models. Such partial inclusive talent management not only helps the organization locate the exact match from the critical mass but also provides an opportunity for the employees to get equal opportunity and feel worthwhile towards various organizational actions and milestones. As a result, there can be a higher probability among such populations to accept, appreciate and contribute toward organizational change initiatives.

In a nutshell, it may be concluded that, across construction industries, where there is a dearth of technically competent manpower, the *'Silent Performers'* should be nurtured with care and developed with a talent inclusiveness approach so that, over time, they can be retained to achieve greater organizational success.

# Chapter 14:

## No Is Not Always Negative!

*14.1. Setting the Context*

Let me take the privilege to ask the readers a few questions that they can easily reflect upon. These questions are pretty simple.

- How many times did you call your relative prior to paying a visit at the weekends and refuse by saying 'No'?
- How do you feel about it?
- Have you refused any relative or neighbor showing interest in visiting you?
- What was their reaction when you said 'No' to them?

The last reflective question is: 'Do you really feel that if the word 'No' is not used, it will make the visitor or yourself comfortable?' The answer is again 'No'. Gone are those days when one or two family members staying in a joint family were available at home to greet the guests.

But in today's fast-changing world with nuclear families and dual-income earners, balancing work and life is challenging. Therefore, weekends are the only time to spend quality hours together, whether by going for a long drive or enjoying a candlelight dinner.

Obviously, dedicated weekends for relatives or friends are usually organized with prior planning. Without any planning, if you drive through a friend's place, there is a high probability that you will find the house closed, and your enthusiasm will turn into frustration or sometimes anger. Using a small word 'No' can save energy and costly mistakes.

### *14.2. Harsh Reality*

Unfortunately, in the daily work scenario, uttering the word 'NO,' particularly to your immediate supervisor, is not only perceived negatively but can also swiftly derive an oversimplified version of you. So, the word 'No' is quite powerful in jeopardizing the image of an individual. However, one question can crop up in the mind of the readers: Why and when do people say 'No'? With a deep dive into the circumstances, you can find some possible answers by setting the contexts when someone says 'Yes' or 'No.'

### *14.3. When We Say No*

There are never-ending occasions when someone says 'No,' and the reasons for them are also never-ending. However, in day-to-day life, we constantly judge stakes and outcomes. Hence, there is a causal relationship between individual risk perception (RPe), which can be high or low and individual outcome perception (OPe), which can again be either positive or not positive. The phenomenon may be present across hierarchies; however, the propensity of saying 'No' is inversely proportionate to the individual career progression and psychometric profiling of individuals. Maybe that is why a student does not refuse the study instruction of a professor even if they deny the instruction. The moment the outcome perception outweighs the risk perception, an individual may not affirm the instruction irrespective of the hierarchy, though there is a significant number of outliers[115]. Our subconscious mind is always trying to maintain the status quo, and therefore, a weighing machine is always balancing the imbalances to equalize the inequalities. The moment the situation is balanced, there is no longer any requirement for a non-affirming statement.

### *14.4. Individual Risk Appetite*

The above phrase is very common in the stock and/or mutual fund markets to offer investors appropriate funds based on the risk appetite. It is defined as the degree of risk an individual or organization is willing to accept or tolerate while pursuing their objectives. It represents their readiness to embrace uncertainty and potential losses in exchange for potential gains. Therefore, if someone has a job offer in their pocket, they can easily say 'No.' As a student of management science, my favourite exercise is to draw a causal relationship, which will allow me to introduce a 2 X 2 matrix again and figure out some possible contexts for when an employee can say the dangerous word 'No!'

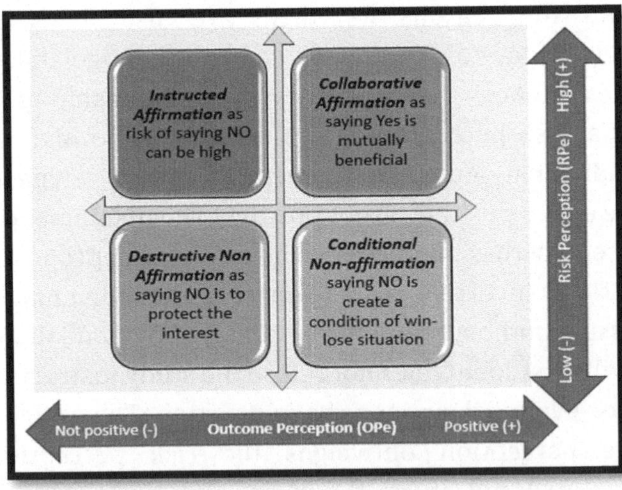


*Figure 14.1: What Is Risk Perception?*

Risk perception is the subjective judgement that people make about the characteristics and severity of a risk. Risk perceptions often differ from statistical assessments of risk since they are affected by a wide range of affective (emotions, feelings, moods, etc.), cognitive (gravity of events, media coverage, risk-mitigating measures, etc.), contextual (framing of risk information, availability of alternative information sources, etc.), and individual (personality traits, previous experience, age, etc.) (Ref: https://en.wikipedia.org/wiki/Risk_perception). It is evident from the definition that the risk for someone may not be perceived as a risk for the other. It is tragic, but most people are conditioned to be judgemental irrespective of education, maturity, age and other personality profiles, and the appetite for listening to 'No' is usually on the lower side.

*14.5. Outcome Perception*

Let me use a small example to clarify outcome perception and how it sometimes works without our knowledge. The outcome of reckless driving for those who drive recklessly can be reaching a destination faster, and for them, risk perception is lower. In contrast, there are some other people whose motto is to drive safely even if they are late for the office; for them, driving fast relates to meeting with an accident, which is a much riskier affair. The outcome perception is the organization, identification, and interpretation of sensory information in each circumstance.

*14.6. Hidden Truth in the Matrix*

Let us have a glance together at the following quadrants to unravel the hidden truth.

- Quadrant I – (Upper left) – RPe > OPe – Higher risk perception associated with lower outcome perception – I believe everyone has faced this situation particularly. If you are being instructed by the visiting CEO to ensure good housekeeping in your department by the next one hour, how will you deal with the situation? What will be your reaction despite your perception that good housekeeping may not fetch a good performance bonus for you? Since the risk perception is far stronger than the outcome perception, the response will be affirmative.

Power distance114 makes the circumstances critical to use the word 'No,' leading to instructed affirmation.

- Quadrant II – (Upper right) – Higher risk perception coupled with positive outcome perception – Just imagine a situation in which your fiancée pledges her request for a costly earring that is beyond your budget. In this critical juncture, anyone can feel the risk perception (here, it is the risk of losing), and, on the other hand, if her request is satisfied, it will positively affect the outcome you want. Saying 'No' can be a costly mistake for you, and therefore, the only option is to affirm.

  Therefore, when RPe = OPe, there is a trade-off, which is a collaborative affirmation for both the people in question.
- Quadrant III – (Lower right) – A positive degree of outcome perception associated with a lower level of risk perception (SPe < OPe) usually leads towards win-lose negotiation since the perceived risk is on the lower side and outcome perception is on the positive end. In the organizational context, most of the top-down instructions are carried out likewise.

  Even employees can use this tactic when they are aware of their skills, competencies, and the market pricing of similar jobs to negotiate with management for higher benefits. The situation leads to conditional non-affirmation.

- Quadrant IV – (Lower left) – Lower outcome perception and lower perceived risk, usually ramified into the loss of faith and mutual harmony at the workplace, are demonstrated through the tussle between the departments and sections with diverse interests. Since both variables are low, there is a good chance of failing any negotiation unless there is the involvement of senior management officials. An organization is not only a conglomeration of people or processes but also a habitation of diverse interests with negotiation power. Our last situation, if not addressed properly, can lead to a situation of destructive non-affirmation, which is nothing but a total collapse of the established procedures.

### *14.7. Summary of the Story*

Finally, let us find out the relevance of the title of the chapter, and let me ask the readers again: Do you really feel that saying no in an appropriate circumstance will portray the image of someone as negative? Ideally, saying 'No' in the right context signals a lack of affirmation, which, of course, is to be substantiated with facts and figures. But, my dear readers, please do not label an individual as negative since they are frequently using the word 'No'.

No means non-affirmative but not negative.

Power Distance – Power distance refers to the strength of a society's social hierarchy. Power Distance Index (PDI) measures the extent to which those at the lower end of the hierarchy accept that social stance or power is not distributed equally in the society. (ref: https://www.organizationalpsychologydegrees.com/faq/what-is-power-distance/)

# Notes

1. ***Bystander View:*** *A person who is present at an event or incident but does not take part.*
2. ***Devil's Advocate:*** *A person who expresses a contentious opinion to provoke debate or test the strength of the opposing arguments.*
3. ***Skill Gap:*** *The gap between the skills required for a job and the skills an employee possesses.*
4. ***Human Capital****: The skills, knowledge, and experience possessed by an individual or population, viewed in terms of their value or cost to an organization or country.*
5. ***Subconscious Mind****: It is part of the mind that is not in the state of awareness. The subconscious mind consists of memories, thoughts, emotions, sensory inputs and habits. It strongly influences individual behavior.*
6. ***Object Referral:*** *The word was coined by the famous psychologist Dr. Karl Jung. It defines us through external objects, such as people, situations, possessions, etc.*
7. ***Job Enlargement:*** *Job enlargement refers to combining job tasks across the same level within a company. Implementing job enlargement widens the scope of individual team members to include more tasks and responsibilities.*
8. ***Development Feedback:*** *Development feedback is a type of feedback that focuses on identifying areas of improvement with the goal of developing learners' skills rather than simply evaluating performance. It provides a mechanism for assessing an employee's performance, a guide for promoting the development of an employee who is trying to master a new task or competency,*

*fodder for self-reflection, and a potential inducement to improve performance.*

9. ***Employee Attrition:*** *Reduction in the number of people who work for an organization that is achieved by not replacing those who leave.*
10. ***Involuntary Attrition:*** *When an employee leaves the company involuntarily. This can happen because of an employee's poor or disruptive performance, misconduct, position elimination, or layoffs due to worrisome economic scenarios. Involuntary attrition is the decision of the company to part ways with an employee and eliminate their position.*
11. ***Superannuation:*** *Reaching the age of retirement.*
12. ***Expatriate:*** *An expatriate, or expat, is an individual living and/or working in a country other than their country of citizenship, often temporarily and for work reasons. An expatriate can also be an individual who has relinquished citizenship in their home country to become a citizen of another country.*
13. ***Furlough:*** *Furlough is a temporary pause in work where employees retain their jobs but are not paid for a specified period. Furloughed workers are still considered employees, but they are forced to take a break from work without pay or to reduce their hours of work.*
14. ***Benching:*** *In the IT Industry, the bench refers to a small percentage of a company's employees who do not work on any project for the time being but remain on the rolls and receive a salary.*
15. ***Voluntary Attrition:*** *When employees leave a company by choice rather than due to factors such as layoffs or termination. This can include resigning to pursue other job opportunities, taking a career break, or retiring early.*

16. ***Functional Attrition:*** *Functional attrition is a term that describes the loss of employees due to incompetence. If employees are unable to meet the job demands due to a lack of essential skills or experience and are unmotivated or disengaged, they can be laid off.*
17. ***Dysfunctional Attrition****: Dysfunctional attrition refers to the loss of valuable employees to the company due to toxic work culture, mismanagement, and low employee morale. This type of attrition can impact an organization's profitability, morale, and productivity, resulting in the company losing experienced staff who are difficult to replace.*
18. ***Upskilling:*** *Upskilling means investing in honing the workforce's existing skills to fill current and future needs. Along with reskilling, upskilling is a crucial component of today's talent strategy.*
19. ***Reskilling:*** *Reskilling refers to the acquisition of entirely new skills.*
20. ***Retention Strategy****: A structured process of handling any dysfunctional attrition by addressing the triggering factors responsible for attrition through mutual dialogue with the employees to ensure that they stay back.*
21. ***Turnaround Time (known as TAT):*** *Turnaround Time (TAT) refers to the duration of a process from leaving the queue to getting completed.*
22. ***Quiet Quitting:*** *Quiet quitting refers to doing the minimum requirements of one's job and putting in no more time, effort, or enthusiasm than necessary.*
23. ***Fringe Benefits:*** *Fringe benefits are additions to compensation that companies give to their employees. Some fringe benefits are universally given to all employees, while others may be offered only to those at executive levels.*

24. ***Performance Incentive:*** *It can be defined as an incentivization by rewarding the achievement of pre-established goals and targets. It can be paid to an individual or a group of individuals based on the rate of achievement of targets.*
25. ***Retention Bonus:*** *It is a payment over and above the fixed salary to keep the key employees within the organization. It is usually paid yearly against their retention.*
26. ***Employee Stock Option (commonly referred to as ESOP):*** *This is an employee benefit scheme that enables employees to own shares in the company. Employees purchase these shares below the market price, or, in other words, at a discounted price.*
27. ***Forced Distribution Method:*** *It is a method of employee performance appraisal that many companies use. We also call it Forced Distribution Method, Stacked Ranking, or Bell-Curve Rating. It is a rating system that employers use to evaluate their workers. Managers must evaluate each employee, usually into one of three categories, i.e., poor, good, or excellent. There may be more categories.*
28. ***Gen Z:*** *Generation Z (often shortened to Gen Z), colloquially known as zoomers, is the demographic cohort succeeding millennials. Researchers and popular media use the mid-to-late 1990s as the starting birth years and the early 2010s as the ending birth years. Most members of Generation Z are the children of Generation X or younger baby boomers.*
29. ***Start-up:*** *The term 'start-up' refers to a company in the first stages of operations. Start-ups may be founded by one or more entrepreneurs who want to develop a product or service for which they believe there is demand.*

30. ***Job Satisfaction:*** *Job satisfaction, an unquantifiable metric, is defined as a positive emotional response one receives while doing the job or being present at work.*
31. ***Solid Citizens:*** *In the context of human resources, a solid citizen is an employee who, despite performing well, reaches a career plateau. This term is sometimes used to describe employees who have been with the company for a long time and have become comfortable in their current position.*
32. ***Organizational Citizenship Behavior (also known as OCB):*** *Organizational citizenship behavior (OCB) is a term used to describe all the positive and constructive employee actions and behaviors that are not part of their formal job description. It is anything that employees do, out of their own free will, that supports their colleagues and benefits the organization.*
33. ***Employee Loyalty****: Employee loyalty is represented as a set of emotions that create a strong bond between the employee and the employer. When the employer and the employee share the same values and goals, mutual trust and respect are established between them, and the employees become interested in staying and promoting the company publicly.*
34. ***Boomerang Employees:*** *A boomerang employee is an individual who leaves a company and later returns subject to the approval of the previous organization.*
35. ***Diversity, Equity and Inclusion (DEI):*** *Diversity means the presence of differences. Equity means fair treatment, access and opportunity for all, recognizing the individual needs of each person. Inclusion means fostering an environment where everyone can feel a genuine sense of belonging and value.*
36. ***Gender Diversity:*** *Gender diversity is equitable or fair representation of people of different genders. It most*

*commonly refers to an equitable ratio of men and women, but also includes people of non-binary genders.*

37. ***POSH Act:*** *Prevention of Sexual Harassment Act came into force to safeguard women from any sexual harassment in the workplace.*
38. ***Replacement Cost:*** *This is the cost of replacing an employee who has resigned or been terminated. It comprises all the administrative and training costs to recruit an employee for a specific role, and the costs are directly proportional to the seniority of the role.*
39. ***Exit Cost:*** *This is the cost that emanates from every voluntary attrition and comprises both monetary and non-monetary exit costs.*
40. ***Operational Cost****: This is the cost incurred due to the disruption in the operational efficiency of the department or organization. It majorly comprises the loss of business or loss of clientele.*
41. ***Work from Home (also known as WFH):*** *Work from home or WFH is a concept in which employees can do their jobs from home using company-approved assets, policies, and tools.*
42. ***Employee Value Proposition (also known as EVP):*** *An employee value proposition is a published statement showcasing the unique benefits employees will receive if they join your business. It explains who you are as a company, your values, and what benefits you can offer in exchange for an employee's time, skills, and experiences.*
43. ***Stakeholders:*** *Typically, stakeholders are investors, employees, customers, suppliers, communities, governments, or trade associations.*

44. ***Grapevine:*** *Grapevine communication relies on messages being spread using informal means of*

*communication (conversations, text messages, etc) which are unstructured.*

45. ***Return on Investment (ROI):*** *It is a performance measure used to evaluate the efficiency or profitability of an investment or compare the efficiency of a number of different investments. ROI tries to directly measure the amount of return on a particular investment relative to the investment's cost.*
46. ***Return on Talent Employed (ROTE):*** *This is a calculation of the ratio of performance to potential for an organization, business unit, or team. It measures how effectively talents are being utilized and whether any of it is going to be wasted.*
47. ***KRA/KPI:*** *KRA is the acronym for the management term Key Result Area, denoting the set of goals in which the management or department aspires an employee to perform. KPI, on the other hand, is the acronym for Key Performance Indicators. It is defined as the metrics through which the performance of Key Result Areas is measured to derive the overall performance levels of an employee.*
48. ***Emotional Intelligence****: According to famous psychologist Joanne Fredrick, emotional intelligence refers to the ability to use, understand and manage one's own emotions in a positive way to manage stress, communicate effectively, de-escalate issues, solve problems and empathize with other people. (https://www.forbes.com/health/mind/what-is-emotional-intelligence/).*
49. ***Employee Advocates:*** *An employee advocate is an employee who supports and promotes their organization, acting as a positive spokesperson and ambassador. Employee advocacy can be a business growth strategy that uses employees for promotion and*

*outreach. Employee advocacy can also mean helping employees become aware of their rights and responsibilities and advocate for themselves when they are treated unfairly.*

50. ***Conformist:*** *A person who conforms to accepted behavior or established practices.*
51. ***Great Place to Work (GPTW):*** *Employers are interested in staying in only those companies or organizations that attract, retain, and engage the right people by unlocking their potential.*
52. ***Dysfunctional Conflict:*** *Dysfunctional conflict is a type of conflict that damages employee relations and hinders organizational progress. It can involve behavior such as aggression, hostility, or lack of respect toward others. Learn the characteristics, examples, consequences, and how to resolve dysfunctional conflict in the workplace.*
53. ***Facebook Workplace:*** *Business focused version of the Facebook which is using the organization platform and used as a tool for the internal communication between the employees.*
54. ***Camaraderie:*** *Camaraderie is a spirit of good friendship and loyalty among the members of a group.*
55. ***Extrinsic Motivation:*** *Extrinsic motivation can be derived by doing something to gain an external reward. This can mean getting something in return, such as money, or avoiding getting into trouble, such as losing your job (https://www.healthline.com/health/intrinsic-motivation#extrinsic-motivation).*
56. ***Intrinsic Motivation:*** Unlike *extrinsic motivation, which arises from outside, intrinsic motivation comes from within. When someone is intrinsically motivated, they can engage in an activity only for enjoyment and get personal satisfaction from it.*

57. ***Career Progression**: Career progression is the process of moving forward in your career. It can take many forms, such as getting promoted, an increase in salary, gaining more responsibility, moving to a different sector or business, taking on new challenges, increasing your skillsets, or starting your own business. Career progression can also mean advancing from one level of a job family to a higher non-supervisory level in the same job family within an agency. Career progression is important because it helps you grow your professional skills and meet your career goals.*

58. ***Self-esteem:** Self-esteem refers to a person's overall sense of their value or worth. It can be used to measure how much a person "values, approves of, appreciates, prizes, or likes themselves" (**Adler & Stewart, 2004**). (https://positivepsychology.com/selfesteem/#What%20Is%20The%20Meaning%20of%20Self-Esteem?).*

59. ***R&R**: Reward and Recognition, commonly known as promoting and motivating good performance by incentivizing the employees through tangible or intangible rewards, are directly attached to the performance achievement.*

60. ***Empathy**: As per the Merriam Webster Dictionary, Empathy is the action of understanding, being aware of, being sensitive to, and vicariously experiencing the feelings, thoughts, and experience of another.*

61. ***Sympathy**: It is defined as he formal expression of pity or sorrow for someone else's misfortune.*

62. ***Anchoring Bias:** Anchoring bias is a cognitive bias that causes people to rely too much on the first piece of information they learn. This information is an anchor or reference point from which all other judgments or decisions are formed.*

63. ***Availability Bias:*** *The availability heuristic is a cognitive bias in which a decision is made based on readily available examples, information, or recent experiences.*
64. ***Egocentrism:*** *As per the Wikipedia egocentrism is the inability to differentiate between self and other. More specifically, it is the inability to accurately assume or understand any perspective other than one's own.*
65. ***Cognitive Bias:*** *A cognitive bias is a systematic pattern of deviation from norm or rationality in judgment. Individuals create their own "subjective reality" from their perception of the input.*
66. ***Overhead Cost:*** *Overhead cost refers to business costs that are related to the day-to-day running of the business. These costs are not directly associated with the creation of a product or service but must be incurred to stay in business, irrespective of the sales level of the organization. Overhead expenses vary depending on the nature of the business and the industry in which it operates.*
67. ***Purchase Power:*** *Purchasing power is the value of a currency expressed in terms of the number of goods or services that one unit of money can buy.*
68. ***E-commerce:*** *Electronic commerce (e-commerce) refers to companies and individuals that buy and sell goods and services over the internet. E-commerce operates in different types of market segments and can be conducted over computers, tablets, smartphones, and other smart devices.*
    *https://www.investopedia.com/terms/e/ecommerce.asp.*
69. ***Gig Economy:*** *A gig economy is a labor market that relies heavily on temporary and part-time positions filled by independent contractors and freelancers rather*

*than full-time permanent employees. Gig workers gain flexibility and independence but little or no job security.*

70. ***SMART Goals:*** *Specific, Measurable, Achievable, Realistic and Time Bound goals.*
71. ***Generation Cohorts:*** *Generation cohorts are groups of people who are born and live at about the same time or during a specific time period. They have similar characteristics, behaviors, ideas, problems and attitudes. Generational cohorts are defined by birth year but not current age because generations get older in groups.*
72. ***Industrial Revolution 4.0:*** *Industry 4.0, the fourth industrial revolution, and 4IR all refer to the current era of connectivity, advanced analytics, automation, and advanced manufacturing technology that have been transforming global business for years.*
73. ***The Bhagavad Geeta:*** *The epic and holy book of Hinduism.*
74. ***Gen Y:*** *"Gen Y" is a term used to refer to the group of people who were born in the 1980s and early 1990s. They are also known as "Millennials."*
75. ***Employee Life Cycle:*** *Employee life cycle refers to the journey of an employee in an organization, from joining to leaving. It is a sequential process that involves various stages, such as attracting candidates, screening them, hiring the best ones, training and developing them, retaining them, and, in the end, parting ways with them.*
76. ***Job Description:*** *Job description or JD lists the main features of a specific job. The description typically includes a person's main duties, responsibilities and working conditions. It also includes the job title and to whom the person holding that job has to report.*

77. ***Employee Experience:*** *Employee experience **(EX)** refers to how employees feel about everything they encounter throughout their employee journey. From the time they apply for a job to the time they leave the organization, their material and relational interactions shape their perception of the organization.*
78. ***Crucial Conversations:*** *Crucial conversations are discussions between two or more people where stakes are high, opinions vary, and emotions run strong. These conversations can affect your life and work and can have negative consequences unless they are handled properly. Crucial conversations are not about confrontation or avoidance but about dialogue, learning, truth, and relationships.*
79. ***Ego:*** *A person's sense of self-esteem or self-importance.*
80. ***Task Orientation:*** *Task orientation refers to the motivational focus on mastering a task. A task-oriented leader, manager, or employee focuses on getting the job done without worrying about the personal development or satisfaction of the team.*
81. ***Relationship Orientation:*** *Relationship orientation is a term that can refer to different things depending on the context. In leadership, relationship orientation signifies the propensity of the leader to approach and focuses on the satisfaction, motivation and the general well-being of the team members before considering the achievement of teams' goals.*
82. ***Idiosyncratic:*** *The word is used against expectations to denote an erratic series of expectations or expectations for which someone does not have any clarity of thoughts.*
83. ***Ethnocentric Bias:*** *Ethnocentric bias (also known as ethnocentrism) occurs when perceptions of others are influenced by the culture of one's own ethnic group. It*

*looks at outgroups and judges them based on the norms and standards of one specific culture.*

84. ***Humane:*** *Having or showing compassion or benevolence.*
85. ***Intelligence Quotient:*** *A number representing a person's reasoning ability (measured using problem-solving tests) compared to the statistical norm or average for their age, taken as 100.*
86. ***Work Ethics:*** *Work ethics refers to the belief that work and diligence have a moral benefit and an inherent ability, virtue or value to strengthen character and individual abilities. Desire or determination to work serves as the foundation for values centered on the importance of work or industrious work. (Source: https://en.wikipedia.org/wiki/Work_ethic).*
87. ***Self-Actualization:*** *Psychologist Abraham Maslow's theory of self-actualization contends that individuals are motivated to fulfil their potential in life. Self-actualization is typically discussed in conjunction with Maslow's hierarchy of needs, which posits that self-actualization sits at the top of a hierarchy above four "lower" needs.*
    *(Source: https://www.thoughtco.com/maslow-theory-self-actualization-4169662).*
88. ***Disengagement:*** *Employee disengagement refers to employees who are less committed to their jobs and the company as a whole. It is the opposite of employee engagement and occurs when employees are less motivated and disconnected from the organization and its mission, vision and goals. Disengaged employees tend to have an apathetic attitude, and they show it in their work by underperforming or by meeting the bare minimum work requirements without any enthusiasm.*

89. ***Moonlighting:*** *Employee moonlighting is a situation in which an employee has more than one job. Usually, the moonlighting employee has one full-time job and one part-time job, though some use the term to refer to a situation in which a person works for more than one company.*
90. ***Secondary Employment:*** *Secondary employment means any external employment or work activity with a public or private entity or self-employment that is in addition to an employee's position with the department, even while on leave.*
91. ***Psychological Contract:*** *A psychological contract encompasses the informal beliefs, ambitions, obligations, and expectations the employee and the employer perceive. Essentially, it is how both parties understand their relationship outside the written and signed employment contract and what they expect the other party to provide. It is typically built on the actions of everyone in the organization, and it strongly influences how employees behave, how organizations respond, and how we manage the employee experience. (Source: https://www.aihr.com/blog/psychological-contract/)*
92. ***Digital Natives:*** *A person born or brought up during the age of digital technology and is familiar with computers and the internet from an early age.*
93. ***Growth Mindset:*** *A growth mindset, as conceived by Stanford psychologist* ***Carol Dweck*** *and her colleagues, refers to the belief that a person's capacities and talents can be improved over time.*
*(Source: https://www.psychologytoday.com/us/basics/growth-mindset#Growth%20Mindset).*
94. ***Baby Boomers:*** *'Baby boomers' is a term used to describe persons born between 1946 and 1964. The*

*baby boomer generation makes up a substantial portion of the world's population, especially in developed nations.*

*(Source: https://www.investopedia.com/terms/b/baby_boomer.asp).*

95. ***SIP:*** *Systematic Investment Plan (also known as SIP) is a plan in which investors make regular, equal payments into a mutual fund or trading account. SIPs allow investors to save regularly with a smaller amount of money while benefiting from the long-term advantages of rupee cost averaging.*

96. ***Cause Motivation:*** *The tendency to be motivated to help the society by engaging in the work associated with it.*

97. ***Non-Compete Clause:*** *A non-compete agreement is a legal agreement or clause in a contract specifying that an employee must not enter competition with an employer after the employment period is over. These agreements also prohibit the employee from revealing proprietary information or secrets to any other parties during or after employment.*

98. ***Cross-Pollination:*** *Cross-pollination in business is the deliberate and strategic blending of ideas, concepts, and practices from diverse sources to foster innovation and drive organizational growth. It involves seeking inspiration and insights from unrelated or seemingly unrelated industries, disciplines, or domains.*

99. ***Behavioral Event Interview:*** *Behavioral Event Interview is a structured and systematic method or approach used to interview potential employees with the aim of uncovering their past behaviors in specific scenarios. In simple terms, BEI can be understood as an interview technique that asks candidates to explain*

*specific situations or experiences from their previous jobs.*

100. ***Psychometric Assessment:*** *A psychometric assessment is used to measure an individual's cognitive ability, personality or behaviors. Often used as part of the recruitment process, psychometric testing provides a fair and objective way of assessing the potential of a candidate to perform well in a job. (Source: https://www.practiceaptitudetests.com/what-is-a-psychometric-test/0.*

101. ***Myers-Briggs Type Indicators (MBTIs):*** *MBTI assessment is the most widely used personality assessment in the world. MBTI framework reveals how we approach the world around us and interact with others, offering insights into our motivation and the motivations of others. This provides a strong foundation for personal growth and development, underpinning enhanced personal effectiveness.*
*(Source: https://eu.themyersbriggs.com/en/tools/MBTI ).*

102. ***FIRO B: Fundamental Interpersonal Relations Orientation™*** *(FIRO®) approach has helped people understand their interpersonal needs and how they influence their communication styles and behavior, improving their personal relationships and professional performance. The FIRO® instrument addresses the core of personality—people's underlying needs—and precisely identifies sources of tension in relationships. (Source: https://asia.themyersbriggs.com/instruments/firo/).*

103. ***Background Verification:*** *Commonly known as BGV which is validation of education, experience and criminal records through the external agency. Through background verification, the prospective employer*

*confirms the information given by the individu.al during the job application, and verifies information like education, work experience, family background, personal identification etc.*

104. ***Succession Planning:*** *Succession planning helps one prepare for future contingencies and ensure that other team members can replace the current employees when they leave the organization or retire. Typically, these succession plans are an integral part of an organization's hiring and talent management strategy. To ensure that you hire the right talent pool, it is essential to frequently review and update the hiring and talent management strategy. The strategy ensures that an organization operates without interruptions after employees leave or retire. (Source: https://in.indeed.com/career-advice/career-development/what-is-succession-planning).*
105. ***Job Rotation:*** *Job rotation is the practice of moving employees between jobs in an organization. These rotations are predominantly lateral, meaning that they happen between jobs on the same level and are not considered promotions. They are also often temporary, with people moving back to their original jobs after a certain time. (Source: https://www.aihr.com/blog/job-rotation/).*
106. ***Augmented Reality:*** *It can be defined as a system that incorporates three basic features: a combination of real and virtual worlds, real-time interaction, and accurate 3D registration of virtual and real objects.*
107. ***Internet of Things (IOTs):*** *According to Wikipedia, Internet of Things (IoTs) describe devices with sensors, processing ability, software and other technologies that connect and exchange data with other devices and*

*systems over the Internet or other communications networks.*

108. ***Talent Exclusivity:*** *Talent exclusivity is a term used in talent management to describe the practice of focusing on a selective group of employees who are considered to be talented while others are considered untalented or inferior in some ways. This approach is supposed to be critical for the effectiveness of talent management. However, it may lead to ethical ambiguity and workforce discrimination, which can have serious implications on the fairness perceived by employees.*
109. ***Delta Change:*** *The expression 'What's the delta?' and variations are commonly used in businesses to refer to the difference between two things or the rate of change between two states, depending on the context. (Source: https://nanoglobals.com/glossary/whats-the-delta/).*
110. ***Distributive Justice:*** *Distributive justice refers to an equitable distribution of benefits and burdens. These benefits and burdens can take the form of income, power, wealth, education, religious activities, and other economic, social, or organizational variables.*
111. ***Managerial Obsolescence:*** *Managerial obsolescence occurs when there is a substantial gap between the requirements of a job and the skills and abilities of the manager to perform such a job competently, primarily because of their inability to keep up with the demands of changing times (Harrison, 2009).*
112. ***Self-Managed Team (SMT):*** *A self-managed work team is a small group of employees who take full responsibility for delivering a service or product through peer collaboration without a manager's guidance. Usually in the assembly line industry self-managed team are present.*

113. ***Experiential Learning:*** *Experiential learning (EL) is, quite simply, learning by doing. We have all learned to walk or talk, not by being shown or told, but by practising and refining our technique. Consequently, trainers and facilitators can implement this method in all sorts of situations with people from all walks of life.*

114. ***Social Learning:*** *Social learning is a theory of learning process social behavior which proposes that new behaviors can be acquired by observing and imitating others. It states that learning is a cognitive process that takes place in a social context and can occur purely through observation or direct instruction, even in the absence of motor reproduction or direct reinforcement.*

115. ***Outliers:*** *In simple terms, an outlier is an extremely high or extremely low data point relative to the nearest data point and the rest of the neighbouring co-existing values in a data graph or dataset you're working with.*

# References

1. Brealey, N. (2017). *50 Psychology Classics* (2nd ed.). Nicholas Brealey Publishing.
2. Burchell, M., & Robin, J. (Year Unavailable). *The Great Workplace – How to Build It, How to Keep It & Why It Matters.* Wiley India Publication.
3. Goleman, D. (2013). *Emotional Intelligence: Why It Can Matter More Than IQ*. Bloomsbury Publishing.
4. Harvard Business Review Press. (2022). *HBR at 100.*
5. Jones, G. R., & Mathew, M. (Year Unavailable). *Organizational Theory, Design & Change* (5th ed.). Pearson Publication.
6. Kahneman, D. (Year Unavailable). *Thinking, Fast and Slow*. Penguin Publication.
7. Maxwell, J. C. (2018). *Developing the Leader within You 2.0.* Harper Collins.
8. Pattanaik, D. (2023). *My Geeta*. Rupa Publishing House.
9. Robbins, S. P., Judge, T. A., & Vohra, N. (2016). *Organizational Behavior: Theory & Practice* (18th ed.). Pearson Publication.
10. Shivakumar, S. (Year Unavailable). *The Right Choice.* Penguin Publication.
11. SME Futures. (Year Unavailable). *Moonlighting in India: Another Work Trend That Is Sparking a Lot of Interest.* Retrieved from
12. https://www.smefutures.com/moonlighting-in-india-another-work-trend-that-is-sparking-a-lot-of-interest/
13. Sussman, D. (Year Unavailable). *Moonlighting: A Growing Way of Life.*

## References

Websites:

1. Oracle. (Year Unavailable). Talent retention: 6 best practices. Retrieved from [URL]
2. Society for Human Resource Management. (Year Unavailable). [URL]
3. Employee Relationship Management Tools. (Year Unavailable). [URL]
4. Forbes. (Year Unavailable). What Is Furlough? Retrieved from https://www.forbes.com/advisor/business/what-is-furlough/
5. Gartner for HR. (Year Unavailable). *Evolve Culture & Leadership for Hybrid Workplace.*
6. Gartner. (Year Unavailable). *Playbook for Future of Work.*
7. McKinsey & Company. (Year Unavailable). What is diversity, equity, and inclusion? Retrieved from https://www.mckinsey.com/featured-insights/mckinsey-explainers/what-is-diversity-equity-and-inclusion#
8. United States Holocaust Memorial Museum. (Year Unavailable). Erwin Rommel. Retrieved from https://encyclopedia.ushmm.org/content/en/article/erwin-rommel
9. University Forum for Human Resource Development. (Year Unavailable). [URL]
10. SME Futures. (Year Unavailable). Moonlighting in India: Another work trend that is sparking a lot of interest. Retrieved from [URL]
11. Medium. (Year Unavailable). 8 Things We Miss on Empathy. Retrieved from https://medium.com/under-30-changemakers/8-things-we-miss-on-empathy-d60287f28138
12. Heartmanity. (Year Unavailable). The three kinds of empathy: emotional, cognitive, compassionate. Retrieved from https://blog.heartmanity.com/the-three-kinds-of-empathy-emotional-cognitive-compassionate
13. Verywell Mind. (Year Unavailable). [URL]
14. ResearchGate. (Year Unavailable). Take a look at life from this window: The Johari Window. Retrieved from https://www.researchgate.net/publication/343970513_Take_a_Look_at_Life_from_This_Window_The_Johari_Window

Others:

1. KPMG. (2022). The Moonlighting Dilemma, October 2022. Retrieved from KPMG website.
2. Sussman, D. (Year Unavailable). Moonlighting: A growing way of life.
3. Gartner for HR. (Year Unavailable). Evolve Culture & Leadership for Hybrid Workplace.
4. Gartner. (Year Unavailable). Playbook for future of work.
5. Shivakumar, S. (Year Unavailable). The Right Choice. Penguin Publication.
6. KPMG. (Year Unavailable). *The Moonlighting Dilemma, October 2022*. Retrieved from KPMG website.
7. Top 5 priorities for HR leaders in 2023.
8. Oracle. (Year Unavailable). Talent retention: 6 best practices. Retrieved from [URL]
9. United States Holocaust Memorial Museum. (Year Unavailable). Erwin Rommel. Retrieved from https://encyclopedia.ushmm.org/content/en/article/erwin-rommel
10. Medium. (Year Unavailable). 8 Things We Miss on Empathy. Retrieved from https://medium.com/under-30-changemakers/8-things-we-miss-on-empathy-d60287f28138
11. Heartmanity. (Year Unavailable). The three kinds of empathy: emotional, cognitive, compassionate. Retrieved from https://blog.heartmanity.com/the-three-kinds-of-empathy-emotional-cognitive-compassionate
12. Verywell Mind. (Year Unavailable). [URL]
13. University Forum for Human Resource Development. (Year Unavailable). Linking Human Resource Development (HRD) And Performance Management: Towards An Integrative Conceptual Framework. Retrieved from [URL]. (Last accessed on Jan 20, 2019)